the new
HARVEST

the new HARVEST

lou seibert pappas and jane horn

Photographs by Renee Lynn
Drawings by Pamela Manley

101 Productions
San Francisco

Text and Cover Design: Lynne O'Neil

Copyright 1986 by Lou Seibert Pappas and Jane Horn
Illustrations copyright 1986 by Pamela Manley
Photographs copyright 1986 by Renee Lynn

Printed in the United States of America.
All rights reserved.

Published by 101 Productions, 834 Mission Street
San Francisco, California 94103.
Distributed to the book trade in the United States by
The Macmillan Publishing Company, New York.

Library of Congress Cataloging-in-Publication Data
Pappas, Lou Seibert.
  The new harvest.

  Includes index.
  1. Cookery (Vegetables)   2. Cookery (Fruit)
3. Cookery (Flowers)   I. Horn, Jane, 1945–   .
II. Title.
TX801.P33   1986   641.6'4   86–1430
ISBN 0–89286–262–9

Cover photograph: clockwise from top center, Belgian endive, leek, red Swiss chard, tomatillo, red and gold bell peppers, oyster mushroom, fiddlehead fern, passion fruit, papaya, kiwifruit, kumquat, pepino.

Frontis photograph I: clockwise from upper left, pomegranate, quince, kumquat.

Frontis photograph II: clockwise from top center, jícama, chayote, cassava, Jerusalem artichoke, fennel, tomatillo, Japanese eggplant.

CONTENTS

ACKNOWLEDGMENTS

We would like to thank the many people who contributed to this book.
  For sharing their expertise: Charles Bettencourt, Sunset Produce; Frieda Caplan, Frieda's Finest/Produce Specialties; Albert Katz, The Broadway Terrace Cafe; Sibella Kraus, Greenleaf Produce; Judy Rodgers; Renee Shepherd, Shepherd's Garden Seeds; Carol Schmidt and Richard McCain, Quail Mountain Nursery.
  And for their participation: Kirby Bennett, recipes; Berkeley Bowl Marketplace, fresh produce; Karen Hazarian, food styling.

INTRODUCTION

America's shopping list is changing dramatically. Nowhere is this change more evident than in the produce departments of our supermarkets. Bins and counters are bursting with almost triple the number of items that were available to us a little over a decade ago. A well-stocked, diversified produce section outranks a quality meat case in consumer priorities, according to industry surveys. Why have fruits and vegetables jumped to the top of our list? The answer: good health, good taste, and good selection.

In response to an increasing awareness of the connection between diet and physical well-being, we are making a sweeping change in our eating habits. To fall into line with current nutritional guidelines, we are turning away from fatty, oversweetened, calorie-laden foods to ones that are lighter, fresher, and more naturally flavorful. Nutrient-rich fruits and vegetables are just what the doctor ordered.

"Fresh" has become a rallying cry for chefs and home cooks alike. This means getting produce from field to kitchen as quickly as possible. Improved methods of cultivation, storage, and transportation have speeded the process as has a dedicated group of small-scale farmers and market gardeners who supply extremely fresh, locally grown crops to nearby restaurants and markets, often planting to order. Farmer's markets, u-picks, and the newer urban phenomenon of street-corner vendors and stands set up near bus stops and train stations are also shortening the distance from harvest to table.

Home and restaurant gardens are sprouting in backyard plots, on windowsills, balconies, and decks as material expressions of our quest to improve the quality of our food. Zesty herbs, succulent lettuces, tiny and tender vegetables, juicy berries, shoestring green beans, and sugar-sweet tomatoes grow within arm's reach of the kitchen. Unburdened by commercial concerns about ease of harvest, good shelf life, and uniform appearance, personal gardeners are free to focus on exceptional flavor and interesting variety as the measures of a successful crop.

Globetrotting American chefs and a recent surge of immigration to this country from Asia and Latin America have created an enthusiasm for regional and ethnic cuisines. Encouraged by our curiosity about unfamiliar and exotic foods, brokers and retailers are gathering an increasingly eclectic and international collection of produce for us to try. Re-examination of our own culinary heritage has also renewed interest in the staples of our grandmothers' cooking. Homey dandelion and turnip greens, rhubarb, Jerusalem artichokes, and kohlrabi are old American standbys appearing in our markets and on the menus of the trendiest restaurants.

With the world farming for us, a greater variety of fresh produce is available year-round. Imports from Europe, South America, New Zealand, Mexico, and Israel, and domestic produce from the warm growing areas of the United States, such as Florida and California, have blurred the seasons; when one source of supply has been just about exhausted, the next is ready to ship.

Professional chefs, always searching for the unusual and rare, are delighted with the diversity of ingredients now available to them: peppers in marvelous shades of gold and purple; scarlet-hued pears and red-skinned bananas; round, plum, and teardrop-shaped red and yellow tomatoes; alligator-skinned tropical fruits that taste like creamy custard, and stubby ones that slice into yellow stars; charming mini and baby vegetables; eye-catching, pungent edible blossoms; and aromatic fresh herbs.

Adventuresome home cooks are eager to follow suit in their own kitchens. Often though, they get no further than the market, stumped when confronted with the profusion of unusual fruits and vegetables before them. They haven't a clue as to how to use them, what they taste like, or even what to call them. Retailers are frequently as much in the dark about these new arrivals as their customers. To help make the exotic familiar and the unusual less mysterious, we've written this guide and cookbook. Let it be your introduction to the new harvest.

the new

HARVEST

vegetables

BEANS

CHINESE LONG BEAN, FAVA BEAN, HARICOT VERT

In one form or another, beans have been cultivated since before recorded history. Fava beans were discovered in archeological sites dating back to the Iron Age; they were prized by the ancient Hebrews, Egyptians, Greeks, and Romans, and were used by the Chinese for food even earlier. A form of green bean was a well-established crop throughout much of Central and South America for centuries before the arrival of the Spanish and Portuguese. Fifteenth- and sixteenth-century explorers carried seeds for this native American variety back to Europe, where it was unknown. In turn, the fava, a staple of the Old World, was introduced into the Western Hemisphere by European colonists homesick for familiar foods.

While the common American bean spread throughout the world, the transplanted fava enjoyed only limited popularity in this country. As Americans become more curious about ingredients from other cuisines and more willing to try them at home, less familiar beans such as favas, French haricots verts, and Chinese long beans, up to now found only in ethnic markets, are becoming more widely available.

PEAK AVAILABILITY August through September.

SELECTION Long beans come in two colors: dark green and pale green. Choose fresh, slim beans that are flexible but not limp, with a dusty matte surface.

STORAGE In a plastic bag in refrigerator crisper 3 to 5 days.

PREPARATION Wash and trim stems if necessary. Cut into 1- to 2-inch pieces, or in desired size. Do not overcook or they will get mushy.

SERVING Use in stir-fries, or in any recipe calling for green beans.

NUTRITION Fair source of vitamin A.

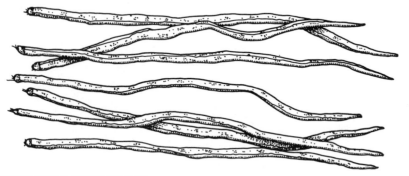

CHINESE LONG BEAN

This oriental green bean has been dubbed the "yard-long bean," a name referring to its unusually long pod. Actually, the nickname is a misnomer, as the beans never quite reach thirty-six inches in length. Its Latin name *sesquipedalis*, which translates to "foot and a half," is closer to the bean's average size. Use these beans as you would green snap beans. Their flavor is similar but milder, with a crunchier texture. The Chinese incorporate the cut-up beans in stir-fries. In the West Indies the beans are used to tie bundles of skewered meat and vegetables. Creative florists in this country use the beans like bows in floral displays.

PEAK AVAILABILITY April, May, and June.

SELECTION Fava pods can be large, ranging from 8 to 18 inches long. Select heavy pods, with a glossy dark green skin, well filled with seeds of equal size.

STORAGE In a plastic bag in refrigerator crisper. Use as soon as possible.

PREPARATION Young pods, up to 4 or 5 inches long, can be eaten raw and whole, simply seasoned with salt. Beyond that size, the beans should be shelled, peeled, and boiled in salted water until tender, about 20 to 25 minutes. Some cooks feel that it's easier to remove the skin if the beans are first blanched and cooled slightly.

SERVING Toss cooked favas in butter and season with salt, pepper, and thyme. Simmer in a soup or stew with Italian sausages and garnish with pesto. Marinate blanched beans in a salad with red or gold bell peppers.

NUTRITION Some vitamin A, vitamin C, and potassium.

FAVA BEAN

The Italians call this lima bean look-alike *fava*, the French *fève*, and the English the broad, horse, or Windsor bean. Its flavor is strong and distinctive. In the spring the tender, immature pods are a delicacy, eaten whole like an edible-podded pea. As the beans develop, they must be removed from the pod, peeled, and cooked. Fully mature beans are dried and often pureed for soups or mashed as a main-course accompaniment.

Favism, a blood disorder aggravated by eating favas or even breathing pollen from the bean's blossom, affects some people of Mediterranean ancestry.

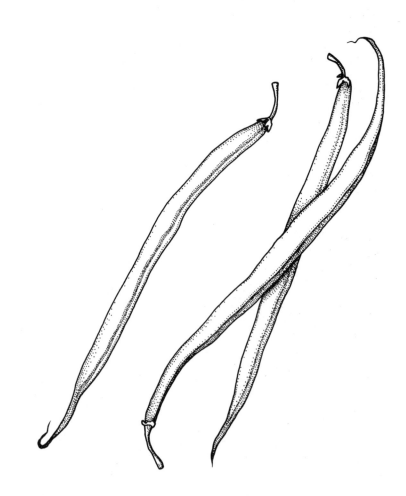

PEAK AVAILABILITY July through September.

SELECTION Buy as fresh as possible; the beans should be very slim (1/6 to 1/8 inch in diameter) with a rich green color. Avoid beans that are limp.

STORAGE In a plastic bag in refrigerator crisper; use quickly.

PREPARATION Wash. Trim stem end.

SERVING These beans need only quick cooking; steam or sauté, drain, and toss with olive oil or butter and seasonings.

NUTRITION Fair source of vitamin A and vitamin C.

HARICOT VERT

Until very recently, French haricots verts—delicate, extremely slim stringless green beans of exceptional flavor—were a rarity in this country. After American chefs tasted these prized vegetables in France, they were eager to use them in their own cooking. Local growers were encouraged to plant them and now restaurants and specialty markets offer these sought-after (and very costly) beans, which can also be easily grown by home gardeners. Seeds for haricots verts are available from companies specializing in quality imported varieties.

CARDOON

PEAK AVAILABILITY October through
December.

SELECTION Buy fresh-looking stalks
that are not bruised or discolored;
the bunch should be compact.

STORAGE In a plastic bag in refrigerator crisper 1 to 2 days.

PREPARATION Discard the outer ribs
as they are often tough and stringy.
Wash and trim off spines. String like
celery, if necessary, by scraping
stems with a paring knife, as the
strings remain fibrous even after
cooking. Cut stalks into 2- to 3-inch
pieces; cook immediately in boiling,
salted water with some lemon juice
added until crisp-tender, about 20 to
25 minutes. When cut, cardoon
browns very quickly. If not using
right away, drop the pieces into acidulated water.

SERVING Drain cooked pieces and
toss with butter, salt, and lemon
juice. Serve as a side dish with a
sauce, or bake with a coating of
bread crumbs and/or cheese. The
Italians coat cut-up cardoon in batter and deep fry, or use the tender
inner ribs raw as a dipping vegetable for bagna cauda—a hot sauce of
olive oil, butter, garlic, anchovy, and
salt. Use cardoon puree as a soup
base. Substitute for celery in salads,
soups, and stews.

NUTRITION Fair source of potassium.

With its deeply scored ribs and spiny, prickly, gray-green leaves, is this
Italian vegetable a mammoth mutant celery? Actually the cardoon is
a thistle and thought to be the ancestor of the globe artichoke. Its flavor is a blend of both celery and artichoke. While the artichoke is
grown for its flower buds, the cardoon is cultivated for the tender,
fleshy midribs of its leaves. Often the plant is blanched to improve the
flavor of the inner stalks by tying up the outer leaves and covering all
with paper for a month before harvesting.
  The Romans used this large and decorative thistle as ornamental
landscaping. According to food writer Waverley Root, pregnant
women in the Middle Ages who wanted to deliver boys consumed cardoons in quantity. Today the cardoon is a favorite vegetable in Italy
and France.

CASSAVA

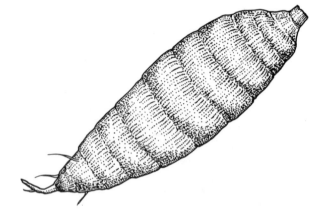

PEAK AVAILABILITY All year.

SELECTION Choose firm, unblemished **sweet** tubers.

STORAGE In a plastic bag in refrigerator crisper 1 to 4 days.

PREPARATION Strip off the peel, slice the hard flesh into 1- to 1½-inch pieces and boil in salted water for 1 to 1½ hours; discard cooking water.

SERVING Latin American cuisines use cassava as a starch, much like yam or sweet potato, often served with fried onions or garlic.

NUTRITION High in starch and vitamin C.

Cassava ranks only behind the potato as the world's leading vegetable crop. This brown-skinned, white-fleshed tuber is an important food for most tropical and subtropical regions of the world. The starchy root is eaten boiled like a potato, or dried and ground into meal, and is the source of tapioca. The leaves are cooked like greens. Other names for cassava, which is thought to be native to South America, are manioc, *mandioca*, and *yuca*.

Most cassava varieties contain poisonous prussic acid to some degree, which makes the root taste bitter. The acid is driven out by heat and so it is essential that cassava tubers be thoroughly cooked.

Brazilians eat the root as a vegetable. Toasted cassava meal—*farinha de mandioca*—is an integral part of their cooking, sprinkled on all kinds of food. In the West Indies cassava meal is called *farine*, in Africa *gari*. Cassareep, a dark, thick syrup made from cassava juice and spices, is the main ingredient in Jamaican pepperpot stew. West Africans use cassava starch for *foofoo*, a sticky, glutinous loaf that is pulled apart and used as a sop for soups and stews.

CELERIAC

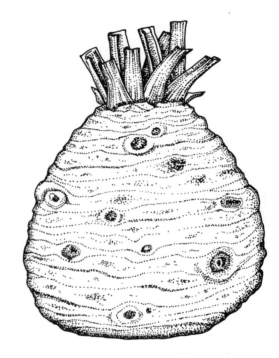

SELECTION Choose small to medium-sized roots about the size of a softball (no more than 4 inches across). Larger ones can be woody and pithy. Avoid any roots that are soft.

STORAGE Trim off tops and rootlets and store in a plastic bag in refrigerator crisper up to 1 week.

PREPARATION Rinse and scrub with a brush. Celeriac is tricky to peel because of its rough surface; a paring knife might work better than a vegetable peeler. Once peeled, it darkens quickly; plunge immediately into acidulated water. If desired, cook the whole vegetable before peeling to prevent discoloration; boil, covered, until tender, about 40 to 50 minutes. Or cook cut-up pieces in a little water until just tender, about 5 to 10 minutes.

SERVING Shred and serve raw tossed in a mustard mayonnaise. Dice and add to soups and stews. Puree and mix with potatoes, a complementary vegetable. Prepare as fritters. Serve as a cooked vegetable with a cheese or cream sauce.

NUTRITION Good source of potassium.

It may not be love at first sight of this knobby, swollen, brown root, with its irregular, coarse skin and tiny, hairy rootlets protruding from its surface. But if beauty is only skin deep, then so is ugliness, at least with celeriac. Scrubbed, peeled, and cooked, the vegetable is transformed into one of great appeal, with a delicate flavor and smooth texture.

Its other names are celery root and celery knob. All suggest its close relationship to celery, which it resembles in flavor only. Unlike celery, its stalks are trimmed away. What is eaten is the swollen base of its turniplike stem, which prompted another of its names—turnip-rooted celery.

Europeans prize this vegetable. Perhaps its most familiar preparation is *céleri-rave rémoulade*, a famous French first course of julienned celeriac marinated in a mustard mayonnaise.

CHAYOTE

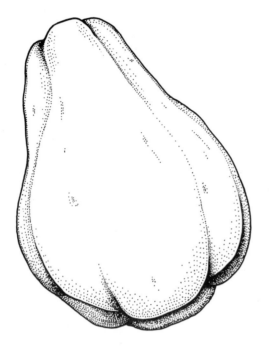

PEAK AVAILABILITY October through April.

SELECTION Choose firm, unblemished squash, heavy for its size.

STORAGE In a plastic bag in refrigerator crisper 1 to 2 weeks.

PREPARATION Peel mature squash; young squash do not need to be peeled.

SERVING Use like a squash. Bake whole or halved, stuffed or plain. Boil or steam until tender, serve halved, in cubes, or mashed, as a hot vegetable seasoned with butter, salt, and pepper. Good in stir-fries. Goes well with carrots, onions, and potatoes, and strong seasonings.

NUTRITION Fair to good source of vitamin C and potassium.

Ribbed, cool green chayote (chai-YOH-tay) is a pear-shaped squash from a prolific tropical vine that can grow up to one hundred feet long and produce as many as two hundred fruits, weighing up to one pound each or even more. The vine is native to Mexico and Central America and was part of the diet of the Aztecs, Mayans, and other Indian cultures long before the Spanish arrived. Chayote is now grown in all parts of Latin America, the Caribbean, Africa, Asia, and in the warmer farming regions of the United States. Around the world it is known as vegetable pear, mirliton, mango squash, *chocho*, and christophine.

Chayote varies in size, averaging four to six inches in length. Its skin is furrowed and smooth, although some varieties have prickly spines. Unlike other gourds, the chayote has only one seed, which is flat and is edible after cooking. Chayote has a mild flavor and a firm texture, which means it doesn't lose its shape when cooked.

DAIKON RADISH

PEAK AVAILABILITY All year.

SELECTION Roots should be young, smooth, and crisp, not flabby, with a good creamy color.

STORAGE In a plastic bag in refrigerator crisper 1 to 2 weeks.

PREPARATION Wash and peel.

SERVING Grate or slice thinly for salads, or as a condiment with pâtés and fish. Use for pickling. Stir-fry, braise, or boil and use in soups and stews like a potato.

NUTRITION Good source of vitamin C.

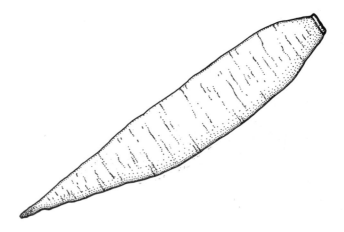

Daikon is the Japanese name for a mildly peppery oriental white radish that grows two to four inches across and anywhere from six to twenty inches long. It is a winter variety, not because it looks like an opaque icicle (which it does), or because it's a one-season crop (it's grown most of the year), but because it can be harvested in the fall and stored over the cold months without losing quality as would smaller salad radishes. Daikon is basic to the Japanese diet, served as a raw or pickled condiment and as a cooked vegetable. It is also considered a digestive aid and breath freshener.

Like all radishes, daikon is a perfect material for carving into fanciful, decorative shapes. In Japan, chefs spend years learning this traditional technique, called *mukimono*. One of their most spectacular and difficult garnishes is a rectangular radish "fishnet," cut in one continuous peeling motion from a specially trimmed daikon. Appropriately, the "net" is draped across seafood dishes.

EGGPLANT VARIETIES

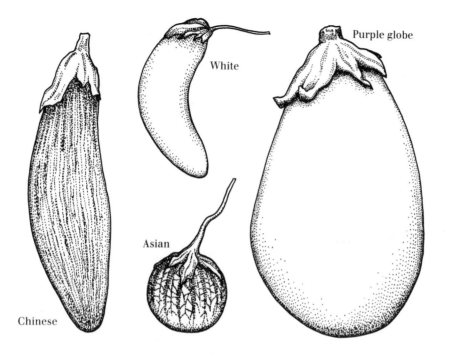

White

Purple globe

Asian

Chinese

PEAK AVAILABILITY July through August. Newer varieties are in much more limited supply.

SELECTION Buy eggplants that are glossy and firm, but not hard, with a fresh-looking cap.

STORAGE In a plastic bag in refrigerator crisper for a few days; use as soon as possible.

PREPARATION Slice off and discard the cap. Peel away skin, if desired. Some cooks salt eggplant slices to leach out bitter moisture (sweet-fleshed Japanese eggplant doesn't need leaching). Slice or cube, and salt each side; let sit in a colander or on paper towels, covered with a weight (a heavy plate works well) for 30 minutes; pat dry and then cook. As eggplant absorbs oil like a sponge when fried, to cook, bake the slices on a lightly greased baking sheet in a 400° F. oven 20 to 30 minutes, turning once.

SERVING Eggplant is part of the French vegetable mixture ratatouille, the Italian relish caponota, and the layered vegetable, cheese, and tomato sauce casserole eggplant parmigiana. In the Middle East, it is *imam bayeldi* (stuffed eggplant) and *baba ghanouj* (eggplant mashed with sesame oil). The Greeks eat moussaka, a casserole of eggplant, meat, and a cream sauce. Brush halves of Japanese eggplant with olive oil and grill until tender. Sandwich a slice of smoked mozzarella cheese between two eggplant slices, dip in seasoned bread crumbs, and sauté until golden.

NUTRITION Not nutritionally significant.

Americans have never been crazy about eggplant. While per capita consumption has slowly increased over the past fifty years, government figures show that even strongly-flavored garlic and spinach sell faster than bland eggplant. So why are more and more varieties of this fleshy vegetable appearing in specialty markets? Probably because cooking today reflects a strong interest in Asian and Mediterranean foods and flavors. Eggplant is an important vegetable in those parts of the world and we are getting a better sense of how to use it.

Although the Chinese and Indians ate eggplant for thousands of years, Europeans shunned it well into the sixteenth century. They considered it poisonous like the tomato, both members of the nightshade family. Italians initially called it "mad apple," thinking it spread diseases and caused convulsions.

In addition to the familiar large, regal, purple globe eggplant, look for long, slender, lavender Chinese and shorter, black-purple Japanese varieties; other types are white or yellow and either round or oval.

FENNEL

PEAK AVAILABILTY September through May.

SELECTION Look for firm, white, crisp bulbs, with white to light green leafstalks and fresh-looking tops; avoid cracked or discolored bases.

STORAGE In a plastic bag in refrigerator crisper; use within 3 to 4 days.

PREPARATION Wash and scrape away any blemishes. Slice and eat raw, or halve or quarter and boil in a small amount of salted water until just tender, 10 to 15 minutes. The sliced bulb can be braised in oil and broth until golden, about 15 to 20 minutes.

SERVING Italians eat the raw fennel bulb and stalks sliced and simply dressed in good-quality olive oil and fresh lemon juice. Marinate sliced fennel and chill with other fresh vegetables and seafood. Blanch, drain, and serve hot with lemon butter. Incorporate in a stir-fry. Use the green tops for a flavoring or garnish. Use the stalks as a dipping vegetable. Serve with fresh goat cheese and fruits, such as oranges and pineapple, in the Italian fashion for dessert.

NUTRITION Good source of vitamin A, vitamin C, and potassium.

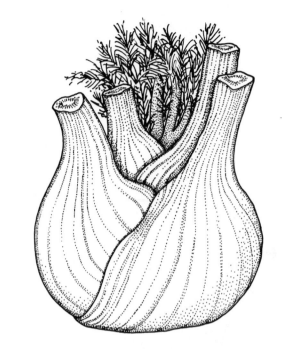

Florence fennel—*finnochio* to the Italians—is cultivated for its bulbous base, eaten as a vegetable. The leaves and seeds of common fennel, another variety, are used as a culinary seasoning. Fennel is native to the Mediterranean region and has been popular for centuries. The Greeks called it *marathon*, after the famous battle site reputed to have been overgrown with fennel. They considered the plant a symbol of courage. Fennel is classic to Italian and French provincial cooking. The seeds flavor sausage, soups, and stews; the leaves and branches are traditionally paired with fish and seafood. In Asia, the seeds are toasted and used as a palate cleanser at the end of a meal.

The overlapping celerylike stalks extend from an enlarged base crowned with feathery green foliage. The base is generally three to four inches in diameter, and may be flat and long or round and bulbous. Fennel has a decisive anise taste when raw; when cooked it becomes more delicate. It is often mislabeled as anise at the market because of its flavor and aroma. Florence fennel is sold trimmed of most of its leaves, and with only a few inches of stalk.

FIDDLEHEAD FERN

PEAK AVAILABILITY May.

SELECTION Choose young, bright green, very tightly curled shoots of the smallest size.

STORAGE In a plastic bag in refrigerator crisper for 1 day.

PREPARATION Remove fuzzy scales by rubbing with fingers or by washing under running water.

SERVING Use raw in salads with a lemon or raspberry vinaigrette. Steam or sauté briefly, toss with butter, and serve as a vegetable. Use sautéed fiddleheads mixed with baby vegetables such as fennel and corn as a garnish for grilled fish or veal.

NUTRITION Good source of vitamin A and vitamin C.

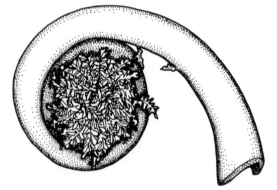

Each spring, the ostrich fern of New England and Canada produces a graceful, tightly curled sprout that in side view resembles the spiral head of a tiny violin. Wild-food enthusiasts consider these coiled tips a delicacy. Fiddleheads are one of those regional foods currently in vogue that delight some chefs and are dismissed as trendy by others.

The ferns are prime when just two to five inches long. Their flavor has been described as a cross between wild nuts and spinach. When properly cooked, fiddleheads have a crunchy texture.

GREENS

PEAK AVAILABILITY All year; particularly plentiful October through April.

SELECTION Choose fresh, green, young leaves with good color; avoid those that are yellow, wilted, or bruised.

STORAGE In a plastic bag in refrigerator crisper 3 to 4 days.

PREPARATION Trim away any roots, wilted, bruised, or discolored leaves. Rinse well under running water. Heavy, fibrous stalks should be peeled or discarded. Cook mature leaves and stems separately. Cut up and simmer in water or broth until tender; braise, steam, or sauté. Also see specific greens.

SERVING Use alone as a vegetable accompaniment with butter and lemon; combine bitter and milder-flavored types. Greens pair well with pork, red wine vinegar, hot red pepper, garlic, butter, and olive oil. Most greens can be substituted one for another; be aware of intensity of flavor as you experiment. Also see specific greens.

NUTRITION Green leafy vegetables are superior sources of vitamin A and vitamin C, iron, calcium, riboflavin, and fiber.

BEET, BROCCOLI RABE, COLLARD AND KALE, DANDELION, MUSTARD, SORREL, SWISS CHARD, TURNIP, ARUGULA, BELGIAN ENDIVE, CURLY ENDIVE, ESCAROLE, LETTUCE VARIETIES, MACHE, RADICCHIO, WATERCRESS

The catchall category of greens includes a wide spectrum of leafy plants eaten raw or cooked. Greens are not new, just newly rediscovered as part of the explosion of interest in regional cooking and an increased awareness of the link between diet and good health. They are homey, strong-flavored, country foods culled from America's South, Italy, France, the Middle East, and Africa, and provide a bonanza of important nutrients. Salads have expanded beyond pale iceberg and tomato wedges to a complex collection of lettuce varieties and other pungent greens garnished with herbs and edible blossoms.

Beet greens   Broccoli rabe

COOKING GREENS

BEET GREENS A special horticultural variety of beet is grown for its leafy tops, rather than the familiar swollen root. Baby and immature beet greens can be cooked whole—leaves with stems intact. Mature beet leaves and stems should be cooked separately. Beet greens are milder than some of the other potherbs. Steam or cook in very little water about 5 minutes, or until tender.

BROCCOLI RABE Also known as *broccoli di rape* and *broccolirab* to Italians who dote on this broccoli look-alike. Broccoli rabe has some buds, but is grown for its leaves and stems rather than large bud clusters, and also has a more pungent and bitter flavor than broccoli. It is popular with young chefs right now, perhaps as part of the growing culinary mania for anything Italian. To prepare, peel away the tough fibrous outer layer of stalk, or cut off stem ends entirely. Use whole, or cut in bite-sized pieces; simmer, steam, or braise.

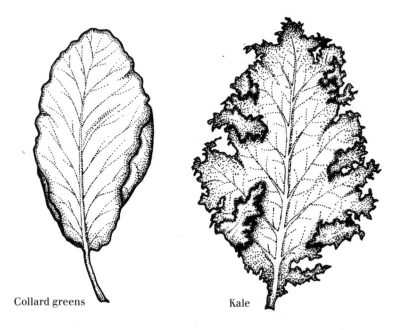

Collard greens   Kale

COLLARD GREENS AND KALE These are the fraternal twins of the populous cabbage family; they are variants of the same plant. Collard leaves are broad, smooth, and dark green. Kale is ruffled and crimped, with a gray-green cast. Curly kale thrives in frosty weather; subfreezing temperature is thought to actually improve its flavor. Collards can tolerate a milder climate and have become synonymous with Southern home cooking. An extremely beautiful form of ornamental kale known as salad savoy is now in the market in soft shades of rose, purple, and cream.

Both collards and kale can be gritty; wash well before using, in two separate baths, if necessary. Cut away heavy main rib sections of collards, then chop the leaves. For kale, strip away the stringy stems and discard. Cut large leaves into pieces. Traditionally, collards are part of a "mess of greens," slow-cooked for hours with ham or salt pork until a velvety pulp. Alternatively, they can be cooked with more "tooth" by simmering in water 15 to 30 minutes. Prepare kale like collards, or steam or sauté. Ornamental kale can be steamed and served whole for a dramatic presentation.

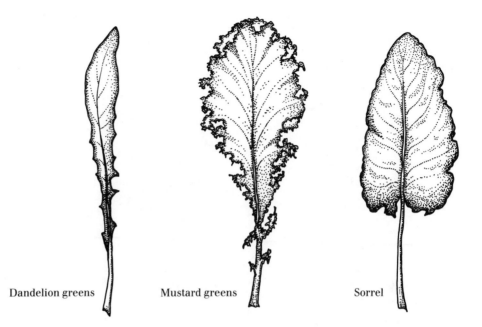

Dandelion greens   Mustard greens   Sorrel

DANDELION This common lawn weed has a long and honorable history in Europe and Asia as a cultivated culinary and medicinal herb, and grew in the kitchen gardens of American colonists. Dandelion greens must be picked young, before the plant has flowered. Mature leaves are tough, fibrous, and bitter. Cultivated greens are milder tasting and are often blanched to subdue the intense flavor. Trim away taproot and wash leaves well. Use whole or torn in pieces for salads; chop for cooking.

MUSTARD GREENS Mustard leaves are one of the more biting of the cooked greens, and may be an acquired taste. Leaves are either frilly or flat depending on the variety. Prepare like collards and kale, mix with other cooked greens, or use sparingly to give punch to a mixed green salad.

SORREL Sourgrass and dock are other names for sorrel, whose acidic, lemony flavor has been described as "sourness incorporated in a green leaf." It grows wild throughout North America and is also grown commercially. Its pleasant tartness balances milder greens, and is used in soups, salads, purees, and sauces, as a side dish, and paired with fish, chicken, and eggs.

Swiss chard

Turnip greens

SWISS CHARD There is no difference in flavor—a blend of bitter and sweet—between the white- and red-ribbed varieties of this foliage beet. The leaves are like spinach, but with a stronger taste and toothier texture. Cook mature leaves and stems separately. Wash and cut stalks into 2- to 3-inch lengths; steam or simmer 10 to 12 minutes, or until crisp-tender. Chop the leaves or cook whole in water that clings to them after rinsing, for about 4 minutes. Serve with lemon butter. Use chard as a poultry stuffing or with pastas.

TURNIP GREENS If you haven't been raised on turnip greens you may *never* develop a taste for them; they can be overpowering. Their assertive tang can be calmed somewhat by combining them with milder greens, or by blanching the leaves before simmering. Use leaves only; the stems are often tough and fibrous. Wash thoroughly. Prepare like collards and kale, in combination with strong seasonings.

Photograph: red and gold bell pepper rings, Anaheim chili (lower left), serrano chili (lower right).

October through April. Some varieties available all year, others in limited supply at times.

SELECTION Choose greens with a fresh appearance and smell, without a droopy, wilted look, or any signs of decay.

STORAGE In a plastic bag in refrigerator crisper for several days; wash just before using. Crispheads keep longer than butterheads and leaf lettuces.

PREPARATION Before using separate from stem. To core iceberg, slam stem end of head on hard surface; core will come out in a plug. Remove core or thick root from radicchio. Wash and dry thoroughly; leafier greens can be dirty. Remove any tough, damaged, or unusable outer leaves. Salad greens should be torn, never cut with a knife, or they will discolor.

SERVING A mixture of greens makes a delectable salad (see How to Make a Green Salad, page 88).

NUTRITION Darker green varieties have good amounts of vitamin A and vitamin C.

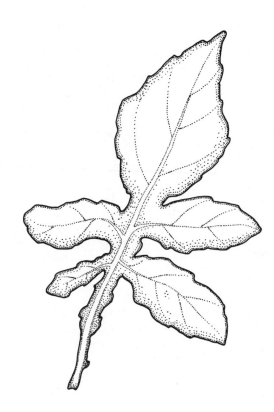

Photograph: mâche on a bed of radicchio, snow pea.

SALAD GREENS

ARUGULA Although associated with the Mediterranean region, arugula—rocket, *roquette*, *rugula*, rocket salad—has been in this country since the first settlers. It was part of the seed inventory carried with the Pilgrims. Peppery and sharp, the small, smooth, notched, dark green leaves are best eaten young, about 3 to 5 inches long; they become too bitter when mature. Also edible are the fragrant four-petaled white blossoms. Trim away roots; wash leaves well as they can be gritty.

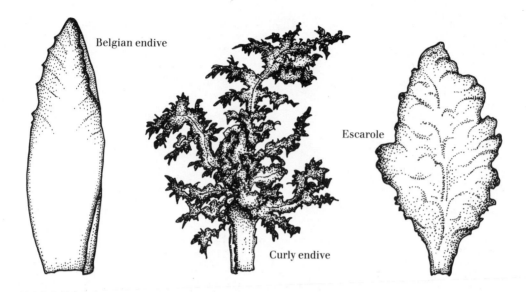

Belgian endive

Escarole

Curly endive

BELGIAN ENDIVE To develop the characteristic whiteness in the shoots, roots for this member of the chicory family are covered with dirt in special forcing beds or removed to darkened rooms for several weeks. Heads are tapered cylinders 4 to 6 inches long and 1½ inches wide, compact with tightly furled, pale, creamy white leaves with yellow shading on the tips. Also called endive, French endive, and witloof chicory, it is mostly grown in Europe, but attempts at commercial production are being made in the United States. Although expensive, one head goes a long way. Store wrapped and use immediately. Wash gently; cut away bitter core with a knife. Use raw leaves whole or cut into rings or fine strips for salads. Fill individual leaves and use as hors d'oeuvres or braise whole.

CURLY ENDIVE This is a frizzy and narrow-leafed, crispy chicory with dark outer leaves and inner ones that are pale to light green, and then yellow toward the center of the loose, open head. Tear off any tough stems; this is a sandy green and needs thorough washing. Use in salads.

ESCAROLE A sibling of curly endive, escarole has broad and wavy rather than curly and flat leaves. The outer leaves are dark green, the center ones a whiter shade. Its flavor, like all chicories, is assertive. Prepare like curly endive.

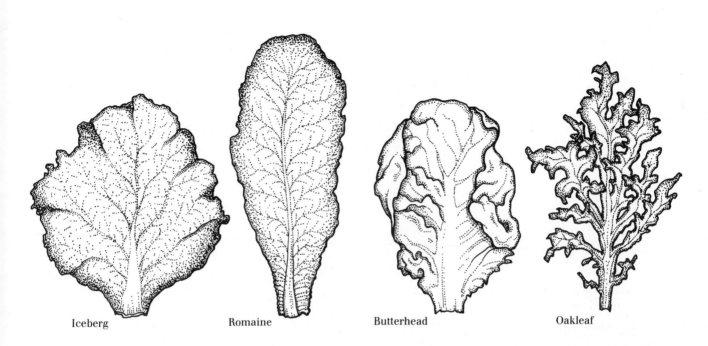

Iceberg   Romaine   Butterhead   Oakleaf

LETTUCE VARIETIES Iceberg lettuce developed into our number-one salad green because it could best withstand the rigors of picking, storing, and shipping to markets across the country from California, a primary source. Improved methods of transportation and storage now allow more delicate (and flavorful) greens to reach markets nationally. Also, local growers are responding to the demand for greater variety by providing wonderfully fresh crops to restaurants and produce markets. Specialty seed companies are supplying seeds for these newcomers so they can be planted in home gardens.

Lettuces are designated crisphead, butterhead, romaine, leaf, or stem lettuce (celtuce). Crispheads—the iceberg—form firm heads of overlapping stiff leaves. Butterheads, including Bibb and Boston, have more pliable heads surrounded by softer leaves that bruise easily, and a sweet and succulent flavor. These are considered premium salad greens. Romaine, also called Cos, has upright, stiff, crisp leaves, with a thick midrib, and a crunchy texture that holds up when cooked. Looseleaf lettuces don't form a head, but grow in rosettes of curly or smooth leaves. Colors range from light to dark green, red, and bronze. Green and red oak leaf, which have indented, flattened leaves, are favorites with chefs and gardeners. Stem lettuce is very uncommon.

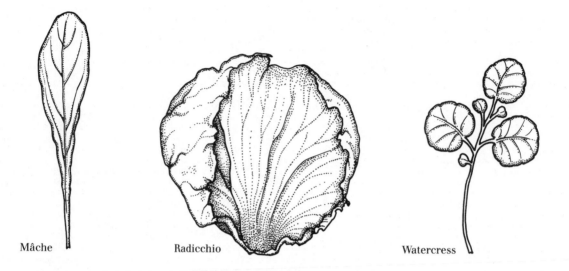

Mâche   Radicchio   Watercress

MACHE Shepherds in Europe named this spring green "lamb's lettuce" and "corn salad," after seeing their flocks nibbling the leaves with delight. Mâche is frequently part of *mesclun*, the French mixture of young greens. Because of its spoon-shaped or round, fuzzy leaves, and mild, nutty flavor, mâche is popular with American chefs, who mix it into daily changing market salads.

RADICCHIO In the Veneto region of Italy, they call this tart, slightly bitter red chicory "a flower you can eat." Several varieties are available in specialty markets: Verona looks like a little cabbage, with a round head the size of a small fist, white stem, ribs, and veins, and reddish leaves; Treviso is slender and tapered, with white ribs and red-purple leaves. Other types are rose-pink, or mottled green and red, with open, loose leaves. Dressed with a simple vinaigrette, radicchio is a favorite Italian salad. The leaves are also grilled and sprinkled with olive oil, salt, and pepper, or dredged in flour, fried, and sprinkled with salt.

WATERCRESS This delicate-looking green actually packs a peppery kick like mustard. It often peeks out innocently from between slices of crustless bread at teas, and also imparts a fresh, clear taste to salads, and sauces.

JERUSALEM ARTICHOKE

PEAK AVAILABILITY October through March.

SELECTION Look for firm, clean, small tubers (about 2 inches in diameter), free of mold.

STORAGE In a plastic bag in refrigerator crisper for a week or more.

PREPARATION Scrub well with a brush to clean away dirt from around all the knobs and crevices; wash thoroughly. Trim away any hairy rootlets. Peel if desired, although the skin is edible. If eating raw, drop pieces immediately into acidulated water, as the flesh darkens when exposed to air; drain when ready to use. The flesh will also discolor during cooking; to keep white, cook in a *blanc*, a mixture of water, lemon juice or vinegar, some flour, and a little butter or oil. Boil or steam until tender, 8 to 12 minutes. Don't overcook, or the vegetable will turn mushy.

SERVING Peel, shred, and use raw in salads. Cook with skin on, peel later, and use in marinated salads, or in a chicken or seafood casserole. Use cooked vegetable like a potato. Puree and serve as a side dish with butter, salt, pepper, and lemon juice, or in soups.

NUTRITION Good source of iron.

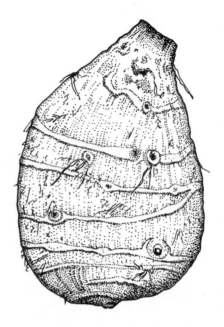

Jerusalem artichokes have an identity crisis. They are neither from Jerusalem nor are they artichokes. They are indigenous to North America, but since the seventeenth century have been more popular in Europe than at home. And finally, when Americans are just getting reacquainted with this small, knobby tuber, it's undergoing a name change at the market to sunchoke.

Going from last to first, Jerusalem artichokes are botanically a sunflower; sunchoke, then, is an attempt to describe the vegetable more accurately. Next, when European explorers reached America, the Indians were growing this species for food. Samuel de Champlain took some tubers (which he described as tasting like an artichoke) back to France in the early 1600s. It slowly gained favor in Europe, while eventually disappearing from American tables until just recently. Finally, Jerusalem is thought to be a corruption of *girasole*, Italian for sunflower.

The lumpy, sometimes branched tubers resemble ginger roots. They have a thin brown or red skin and creamy white flesh. The flavor is delicate and nutty when raw, with a crunchy texture. Cooked, sunchokes become softer, like a potato, and sweeter.

JICAMA

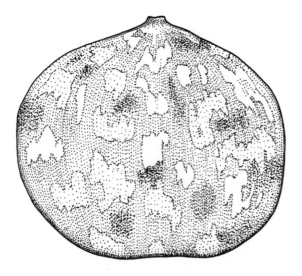

PEAK AVAILABILITY October through May.

SELECTION Choose firm, well-shaped tubers, free from blemishes and relatively heavy for their size.

STORAGE In a plastic bag in refrigerator crisper 1 to 2 weeks.

PREPARATION Peel off the thin outer skin and the layer of white fibrous flesh just beneath it.

SERVING Cube raw jícama, season with salt and ground red chili pepper, and serve with a squeeze of lime as an hors d'oeuvre. Serve jícama sticks with guacamole or other dips. Include raw jícama as part of a fruit salad. To cook, treat like a potato: steam, boil, bake, or mash. Slice and stir-fry with beef, pork, chicken, or shrimp; combine and stir-fry with water chestnuts and shiitake mushrooms.

NUTRITION Fair source of vitamin C.

Although consumers may mispronounce its name (HEE-kama is correct), they've clearly taken to this Mexican root vegetable because of its marvelous sweet crunch. Los Angeles produce wholesaler Frieda Caplan predicts that jícama will soon move out of the specialty category and become as familiar to American shoppers as fresh mushrooms.

Jícama, which looks like a flattened turnip, is the tuber of a tropical morning glory vine. The vine's beautiful, large white or blue blossoms are pinched off as buds to encourage development of the roots, which can weigh from one to six pounds. Its crisp white flesh resembles a cross between a water chestnut and potato. Unlike celeriac and Jerusalem artichoke, jícama doesn't darken when cut. It is a perfect substitute for more expensive water chestnuts in stir-fries.

KOHLRABI

PEAK AVAILABILITY May through November; most plentiful in June and July.

SELECTION Choose small to medium bulbs (golf ball to baseball sized). Avoid anything larger, as they will be tough, fibrous, and bitter.

STORAGE In a plastic bag in refrigerator crisper about 1 week.

PREPARATION Very young bulbs don't have to be peeled. If purchased young with leaves attached, trim leaves and cook separately; they have a delicate cabbage flavor. Peel root, cut up, and serve raw. Or slice or cube, and steam or boil until crisp-tender, about 10 to 15 minutes.

SERVING Slice and use raw in salads, or as a crudité with a dip. Serve cooked root with butter and seasonings or with a sauce; use whole or pureed in soups and stews. Add to stir-fries. Steam tender leaves and drizzle with butter and lemon juice.

NUTRITION Excellent source of vitamin C and potassium.

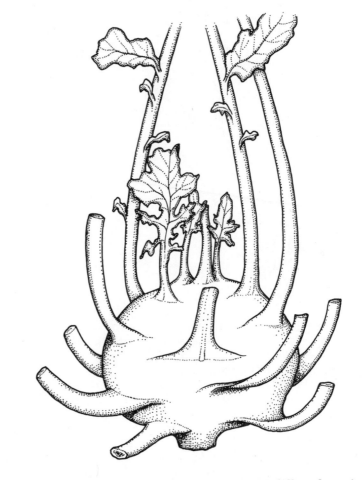

Similar to a turnip in size and shape, kohlrabi differs from its look-alike in that it's actually a bulbous stem, not a root. Both are cabbage relatives, but in different subgroups. It's a peculiar-looking thing, light green or purple, with leaf stalks growing up from all sides instead of in a bunched group. The name means "cabbage turnip," from the German *kohl* (cabbage), and *rabi* (turnip). The flavor hints of both vegetables.

Kohlrabi is common in central Europe and Asia, and integral to German and eastern European cuisines.

LEEK

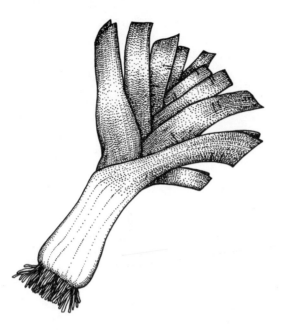

PEAK AVAILABILITY September through April.

SELECTION Choose young, small leeks that are white 2 to 3 inches from the roots, with fresh-looking, vivid green tops.

STORAGE In a plastic bag in refrigerator crisper 3 to 5 days.

PREPARATION Because leeks are blanched (covered with dirt during the last month or so of their growth to stay white), sand and grit get imbedded between the tightly rolled leaves. Wash thoroughly. Remove the tough outer leaves and all but 2 or 3 inches of green tops, cut off the roots, and split the stalk in half to expedite cleaning. Separate leaves and soak in cold water. To clean the stalk whole, make slits around the stalk and hold under cold water. Cooking time depends upon the size of the vegetable. Simmer whole 12 to 18 minutes. Or, blanch, then braise 8 to 15 minutes.

SERVING Slice and use raw in salads. Leeks make wonderful soups and stews like Scottish cock-a-leekie, or pureed with potatoes for vichyssoise. Italians bake leeks in a savory tart or braise them in wine or stock and serve with seasoned butter as a main-dish accompaniment.

NUTRITION A good source of potassium and fair source of vitamin C.

An American cookbook from the early part of this century instructed its readers not to be "prejudiced against the leek because of its relationship to the onion family. It has not a pronounced onion flavor; it is sweet, bland, and its aroma is decidedly pleasant." European cooks would be puzzled by such a caution. They've used this aristocratic vegetable for centuries in soups, tarts, or braised as an accompaniment.

The lore and history surrounding leeks is as old as civilization. Egyptians and Greeks prized the leek, still a favorite in Mediterranean countries. Nero, the Roman emperor, suposedly ate these plump bulbs to improve his voice. Leeks have been prescribed as a cough medicine, a cure for nosebleeds and hemorrhoids, and as a rejuvenating tonic. The Welsh consider this plant their national emblem. During a critical battle in 640 A.D., Welsh soldiers wreathed their helmets with leeks to distinguish themselves from the enemy, and to avoid shooting one of their own. The Welsh were victorious.

The leek resembles a giant, fortified scallion, with its overlapping leaves, green at the top and white at the bulb, and bearded roots. The white bulb and pale yellow inner leaves are considered the most desirable for eating.

MUSHROOMS

PEAK AVAILABILITY Some kinds are available all year, but peak season is October through January.

SELECTION Look for firm, fresh-looking specimens, without moisture or rot.

STORAGE Refrigerate, loosely wrapped. Store mushrooms in an open container, perhaps draped with a damp paper towel, as they need air and humidity. Use within a day or two for optimum quality.

PREPARATION Wash or wipe clean; dry thoroughly. Trim away tough stem ends.

SERVING Most do best with simple preparation. As some wild mushrooms can cause stomach upsets if eaten raw, to be on the safe side, cook first.

NUTRITION Good source of potassium.

CHANTERELLE, ENOKI, HEDGEHOG, KING BOLETE, MATSUTAKE, MOREL, OYSTER, SHIITAKE

As part of our broadening culinary focus, exotic mushrooms—both wild and cultivated—are appearing more frequently in specialty produce markets. Many are hand-gathered from forests and fields by professional mycologists. Others are being grown commercially in controlled environments. Wild mushrooms available fresh include: bolete, chanterelle, matsutake, morel, and hedgehog. Cultivated types are: enoki, oyster, and shiitake.

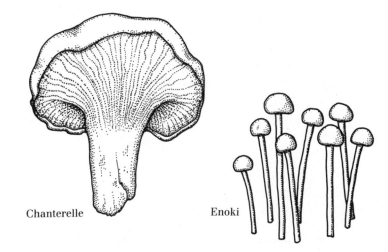

Chanterelle   Enoki

CHANTERELLE In France they are *girolle*, in Germany *pfifferling*, in any language "delicious." Chanterelles have a showy orange color and look like delicately ribbed trumpets. In flavor and odor these wild mushrooms resemble apricots.

ENOKI Its full name is enokitake, meaning "mushroom of the huckberry tree." A favorite in Japan and second only to the shiitake in cultivation there, it grows in clumps of creamy white spaghettilike strands. Each strand is topped with a little button cap. Although bland in flavor, enoki lends a crispness and charm to salads and stir-fry dishes.

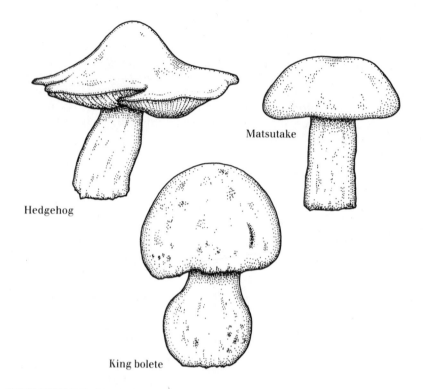

Matsutake

Hedgehog

King bolete

HEDGEHOG Orange to cream-colored, these are "teeth fungi," so called because of the teethlike spines that hang from the underside of the cap. This wild mushroom has a firm texture like the chanterelle and a mild flavor. It can be used interchangeably with other mushrooms.

KING BOLETE *Cèpe* in France, and *porcini* in Italy, this is definitely an aristocrat, ranking with the morel as one of the finest of wild mushrooms. Pair with mild flavors. Classically prepared as a sauté with butter, garlic, and parsley, or with olive oil and shallots.

MATSUTAKE These brownish pine mushrooms are native to Japan. They are so highly sought after there that city dwellers rush to the countryside in the fall to collect them, carrying pots so they can cook and eat them in the woods. In America, Japanese immigrants discovered a white matsutake in the forests of the Pacific Northwest. It has a lively, spicy flavor, and is good marinated and grilled, or steamed.

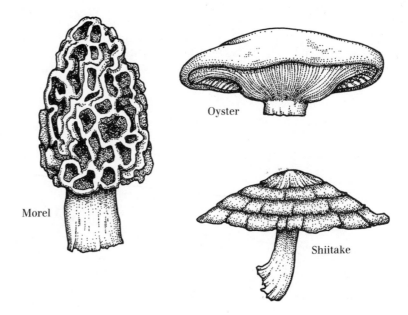

Morel

Oyster

Shiitake

MOREL To many connoisseurs, these wild mushrooms are the finest. They grow two to six inches tall, with a distinctive pitted, pale golden or black spongelike cap attached to a creamy stem; they are hollow from top to bottom. Their earthy, smoky flavor and woodsy scent are showcased best when paired with subtle flavors.

OYSTER Cultivated and wild, oyster mushrooms grow on decaying logs of dead or failing hardwood trees in a characteristic overlapping pattern. They come in various shades of gray to cream, have white flesh and gills, and little, if any, stem. Called the "shellfish of the forest," they have a strong, pleasant odor and taste, and pair well with veal, pork, poultry, or game.

SHIITAKE Although a wild mushroom, shiitakes have been grown for thousands of years by the Chinese. Today, they are also farmed in Japan and in this country. To produce, holes are drilled in water-soaked logs of hardwood trees, particularly oak, and filled with shiitake spawn. The mushroom has a meaty, intense flavor, and is grilled whole, sliced and sautéed, or used in sauces.

PEAS

SNOW PEAS, SUGAR SNAP PEAS

Peas fall into two categories: the garden type, which must be removed from the pod to eat, and those we can eat pod and all. We all love fresh garden peas, but who loves to shell them? Edible-podded peas make everyone happy; we can enjoy their clean, bright flavor without having to work hard. The French call these peas *mangetout*—"eat it all." Two varieties are now in the market.

PEAK AVAILABILITY All year; most plentiful May through September.

SELECTION Pick young, small pods, with a good green color and barely visible peas.

STORAGE In a plastic bag in refrigerator crisper; use quickly.

PREPARATION Wash. Remove the string by pulling back on stem; the top string will come right off. Repeat with bottom string, if desired. Snow peas are good raw, but brief blanching enhances the bright green color and crisp texture and should be done if peas are to be used as a crudité. To blanch, drop in boiling water less than 1 minute and refresh in cold water to stop the cooking process; drain. To cook, sauté quickly in a little oil 1 to 2 minutes. Add as the last ingredient in stir-fries. Do not overcook, or the pods will turn gray-green and mushy.

SERVING Serve raw as a snack. Blanch and toss with water chestnuts, chicken, and a sesame dressing. Split and fill with herbed cheese as an hors d'oeuvre. Use in stir-fries.

NUTRITION Fair amounts of vitamin A and vitamin C.

SNOW PEAS

Also called sugar peas, these are flat, thin-skinned, and tapered at both ends, with tiny peas visible through the translucent pod. They are a familiar vegetable in Chinese stir-fries, and when blanched, slit, and stuffed, a popular finger food. Previously only available in Asian markets or frozen, fresh snow peas are now in most supermarkets.

PEAK AVAILABILITY February through September.

SELECTION Pick plump, round, bright green pods, well-filled with peas of even size.

STORAGE In a plastic bag in refrigerator crisper; use as soon as possible.

PREPARATION Wash. String by pulling back from stem end; string bottom, if desired. Use whole or snap in pieces. To cook, blanch briefly in boiling water, or steam 5 minutes, or sauté in oil or in a combination of oil and butter 1 to 2 minutes.

SERVING Enjoy raw, or lightly cooked as a side dish.

NUTRITION Fair amounts of vitamin A and vitamin C.

SUGAR SNAP PEAS

This is the almost perfect pea—a cross between the garden variety and the snow pea. It was developed by an Idaho horticulturalist and introduced in 1979. Home gardeners were delighted with its sweet flavor, rushing guests from front door to backyard to try one right off the vine. Sugar snap peas are now found in specialty produce markets and well-stocked supermarkets.

PEPPERS

SWEET, CHILI

Hundreds of varieties of edible peppers grow worldwide. About 90 percent of them are hot chilies, with the rest falling into the sweet pepper category. They were grown in the Americas long before the arrival of Christopher Columbus, who mistakenly thought he had found a new source for the prized Asian peppercorn when he reached the New World. Because of their fiery taste, he named this fruit *pepper* anyway.

PEAK AVAILABILITY Sweet peppers are available all year, with a peak from May to November. Red peppers are most plentiful in the fall, although imports from Europe and Mexico have expanded their season. Chili peppers are in season from midsummer to fall; imports allow these peppers to be available other times of the year as well.

SELECTION Look for deep, glossy color and firm, thick flesh, with no cracks or bruises. Chili peppers should be richly colored; paleness is a sign of immaturity.

STORAGE Refrigerate peppers in a pierced plastic bag in crisper; use within a few days.

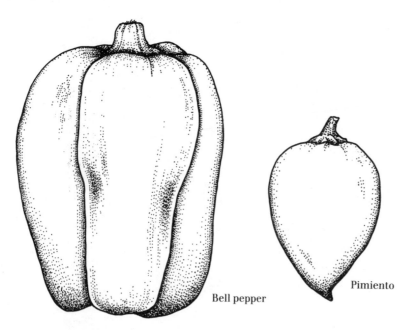

Bell pepper

Pimiento

SWEET PEPPERS

The most common sweet pepper is the familiar blocky bell, which is green to maturity and then further ripens to bright red. When green it has a mild, grassy flavor which sweetens and mellows as the flesh reddens. Other colors have been introduced from Europe. Gold peppers, which are imported from Holland and are also grown in California, start off green and develop yellow skin and flesh when mature. Purple-skinned peppers have green interiors. When cooked they lose their novel color and fade to khaki. Other sweet peppers are heart-shaped pimientos, previously reserved for processing, but now available fresh, and long, tapering European types.

PREPARATION Most recipes call for peppers to be cored and seeded. Depending on the recipe, slice, cube, or dice. Always wear gloves when handling hot peppers. Chilies can burn the skin. Never touch your face or eyes, and wash hands thoroughly.

To roast and peel peppers: Char over a flame on all sides, or broil until skin blisters and blackens. Sweat in a paper or plastic bag 15 to 20 minutes. The skin will pull away.

SERVING Beautifully colored sweet peppers add a bright accent and fresh flavor to salads, stews, and soups. Red and yellow peppers hold their color when cooked; green and purple become khaki. Stuff bell pepper shells with rice and meat and bake until tender, or fill with a chicken or seafood salad. Roast and peel red, yellow, and green peppers; core, seed, and slice. Toss with olive oil, lemon juice, salt, and pepper for a wonderful salad. Hot peppers make a zestful addition to appetizer spreads, and star in a wide range of ethnic dishes—Mexican, Indian, and oriental.

NUTRITION Peppers contribute vitamin A and vitamin C, the former increasing as the pepper becomes warmer in color.

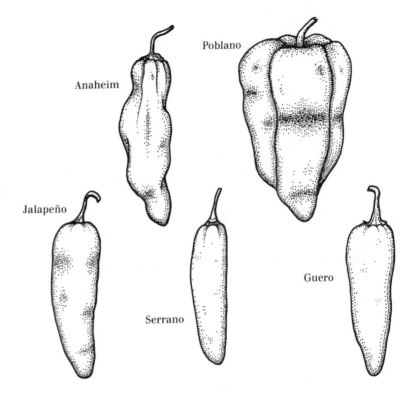

CHILI PEPPERS

Capsaicin is the fuel that puts the fire in hot peppers. This alkaloid substance is in the chili's veins, seeds, and ribs. Innumerable kinds of chili peppers exist. Within each type are many subtypes. The hotness of each is affected by climate, weather, and soil conditions, which means that a chili that grows hot in the desert Southwest will be less incendiary when planted where it is cooler and wetter. Common hot peppers include: Anaheim (or California when dried), long and green, mildly hot; poblano (or ancho when dried), dark green and stocky, medium-hot; jalapeño, small, green or red, and hot; serrano, pale green and smaller than the jalapeño, and very hot; Fresno, the size of a jalapeño, red, and very hot; Guero and Caribe: like a jalapeño in size and shape, yellow, and very hot.

SPAGHETTI SQUASH

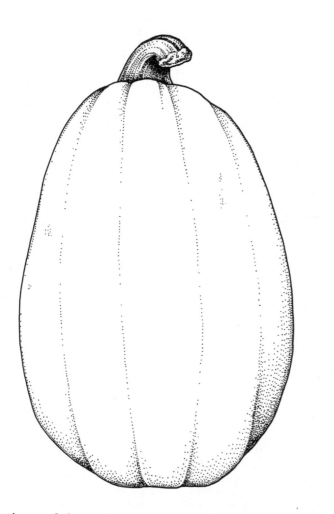

PEAK AVAILABILITY September through December.

SELECTION Look for firm, unblemished rinds. Spaghetti squash ranges from 2 to 5 pounds.

STORAGE In a cool, dry place 1 to 2 weeks; like all winter squash, it doesn't have to be refrigerated.

PREPARATION Cook whole in boiling water, or halve and steam, or bake whole or halved. Timing depends upon the size of the squash. For a 3-pound squash, split in half, scoop out seeds, and place squash, cut side down, in a baking dish. Add water to a depth of 1 inch. Bake in a 375° F. oven 45 to 55 minutes, or until squash is tender when pierced with a fork. Or place halved squash in a large saucepan; add water to a depth of 2 inches. Simmer, covered, 30 to 40 minutes, or until squash is crisp-tender; drain. Remove from pan and fluff with a fork.

SERVING Use like a pasta sautéed with other ingredients and seasoned with herbs. Serve with browned butter, Italian meat sauce, pesto sauce, or a fresh tomato and mushroom sauce. In soup add to broth as the last ingredient and cook just until heated. Serve cold, marinated in a salad.

NUTRITION Good source of vitamin A, vitamin C, and potassium, and a fair source of iron.

Spaghetti squash has to be seen to be believed. On the outside, this oval, golden yellow gourd is hard shelled, like other winter squash. When cooked, however, instead of having the expected firm consistency, its interior fluffs and separates into pastalike strands. One cooking teacher says that when he includes spaghetti squash as part of a winter menu class, there are always a few students who insist the strands were hand-cut while their backs were turned.

All year; supplies of some varieties are limited and irregular.

SELECTION Choose crisp, fresh sprouts without any brown or slimy spots.

STORAGE In a plastic bag in refrigerator crisper 2 to 3 days. Sprouts (except for bean sprouts) benefit from a daily sprinkling of water while refrigerated.

PREPARATION Rinse before serving. Sprouts are ready as is; there is no need to pull off their loose hulls.

SERVING Serve bean sprouts in salads, in stir-fried dishes, or in omelets. Incorporate more delicate sprouts like alfalfa and clover in salads, sandwiches, and as garnishes.

NUTRITION Fiber, vitamin C, and vitamin A.

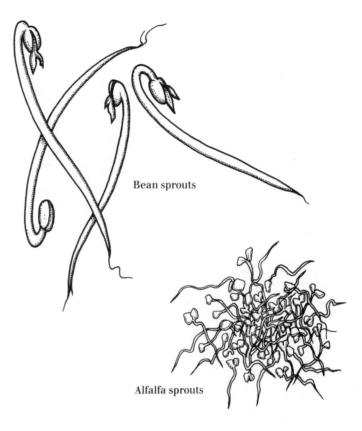

Bean sprouts

Alfalfa sprouts

The sprouts of beans and seeds add fresh flavor and crisp texture to stir-fried dishes, sandwiches, and salads. Sprouted mung beans are a staple in oriental cuisine. Health food enthusiasts and vegetarians have long appreciated alfalfa sprouts as an exotic substitute for lettuce. Now both bean sprouts and alfalfa sprouts are widely available in supermarkets, and other varieties are being introduced on a limited basis.

Look for sweet and peppery clovers, giant, nutty sunflower sprouts, and spicy kiaware (daikon radish sprouts). Sprouts are sold prepackaged or loose.

TOMATILLO

PEAK AVAILABILITY August through November.

SELECTION Sizes range from grape to lemon. Choose firm, unblemished specimens; colors can be pale green, yellow, or purple-tinged.

STORAGE With husks on in a plastic bag in refrigerator crisper for 1 week, or in a cool, dry, airy spot for a month or more.

PREPARATION Peel off husks and rinse. To cook, place in boiling water to cover, reduce heat, and simmer 5 to 10 minutes, or until just tender.

SERVING Slice and use raw in salads. Cook and use in meat or vegetable stews, or in sauces.

NUTRITION Good source of vitamin C.

This lemony-tasting vegetable resembles a small green tomato encased in a papery husk. Although often confused with the tomato, the two are not interchangeable, as the flesh of tomatillos (toh-ma-TEE-os) is firmer. Tomatillo is a husk tomato relative of the ground cherry and cape gooseberry, but unlike those fruits, fills its husk completely.

A native of Mexico, the tomatillo is widely used in that country's cuisine, serving as a main ingredient in salsa verde, the spicy green relish lavished on tacos, enchiladas, and other cooked foods, and in stews.

TRUFFLE

PEAK AVAILABILITY The season for imported truffles varies from year to year. White truffles are generally available from October through early December, and black truffles from January through mid-February.

SELECTION Size varies from a peppercorn to a potato with the average being walnut-sized. Look for aromatic, plump, well-formed ones without bruises or abnormal color.

STORAGE Use immediately, or store in a glass jar cushioned on a bed of rice, or place amid eggs in their shells (the eggs will absorb some of the truffle flavor).

PREPARATION Gently wash and peel off skin; save peelings and use to flavor sauces.

SERVING Thinly slice and use raw or cooked in pâtés, omelets, sauces, pastas, risotto, and veal entrees. Truffles are used as a garnish; special decorative cutters are available at well-stocked cookware stores. Only a small amount of truffle is need to infuse any dish with its flavor.

NUTRITION Not determined.

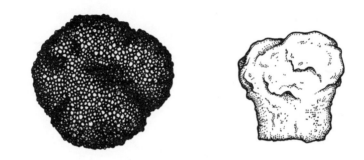

French gastronome Brillat-Savarin described the truffle as "the diamond of the art of cookery." Like diamonds, this subterranean fungus is rare and costly, with price tags reaching hundreds of dollars per pound. While truffles are found around the world, the Périgord region of France is considered the premier source for black truffles. Piedmont, in northern Italy, supplies a sought-after white variety. Truffles have by and large resisted commercial cultivation, but, not surprisingly, efforts to grow them persist. The French were successful on a small scale in the late 1970s, and attempts are now being made in California and Texas.

Truffles develop in symbiosis with tree roots, especially those of oaks. They receive nutrients from the tree, and in turn provide their host with water and minerals from the soil. As truffles never grow above ground, hunters rely on specially trained pigs and dogs who are attracted to the truffle's musky scent. Scientists speculate that the odor is sexually stimulating to the animals, who must be pulled away from the site before they can eat the fungus themselves. This may give some credibility to the long-held myth that truffles are an aphrodisiac. Napoleon reportedly fathered his only son after eating this delicacy.

WATER CHESTNUT

PEAK AVAILABILITY All year.

SELECTION Choose fresh, firm corms.

STORAGE Refrigerate, unpeeled; use within 5 days.

PREPARATION Wash and peel raw. If desired, blanch before peeling; the skin will come off easier. If not using immediately, after peeling drop into acidulated water to hold color.

SERVING Slice or dice and use in salads, omelets, soups, stews, and stir-fry dishes.

NUTRITION Good source of potassium.

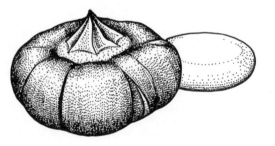

In the Orient and Southeast Asia, this rushlike aquatic plant often grows in marshes in rotation with rice. The edible part of the plant is the brown or black corm, valued for its white, slightly sweet, nutty flesh which stays crisp when cooked.

At the market, water chestnuts look like little flower bulbs, with a brown-black skin. Although it is more work to peel fresh ones than to open a can, their flavor and texture are superior and worth the extra effort.

the new

HARVEST

fruits

ASIAN PEAR

PEAK AVAILABILITY September through December.

SELECTION Fresh fruits, free of bruises.

STORAGE In a plastic bag in refrigerator crisper up to 1 month.

PREPARATION If using with peel, wash first.

SERVING The pears are best eaten chilled. Serve raw, with or without skin, thinly sliced or in wedges, with a twist of lemon or lime. Mix into fruit, vegetable, or main-course salads. Poach and serve as an accompaniment during the meal, or as dessert.

NUTRITION Fair source of vitamin A, vitamin C, and fiber.

Although also called apple-pear because it blends the pear's juicy sweetness and bouquet with the crisp texture and round shape of an apple, this fruit is really a true pear. Many varieties exist: some are more applelike, others closer to pears; some have skins that are russeted and relatively thick, while others are greenish-yellow and thin-skinned.

Asian pears are ready to eat when you buy them, and depending on variety can have an amazing shelf life—a month or more in the refrigerator. Other plusses include a firm consistency even when cooked, and an affinity for other fruits, which makes them ideal for salads.

CAPE GOOSEBERRY

PEAK AVAILABILITY March through June.

SELECTION Choose fruit with un-damaged husks.

STORAGE Ripe when sold; refriger-ate in a plastic bag in crisper 1 to 2 days.

PREPARATION Peel away husk; rinse fruit.

SERVING Serve raw in a fruit salad. Use in a sauce as topping for ice cream or sorbet. Cook with other fruits in a compote. Mix with apples, dried apricots, bread crumbs, and nuts as a savory stuffing for chicken or pork. Make into jam or preserves.

NUTRITION Good source of vitamin A and vitamin C.

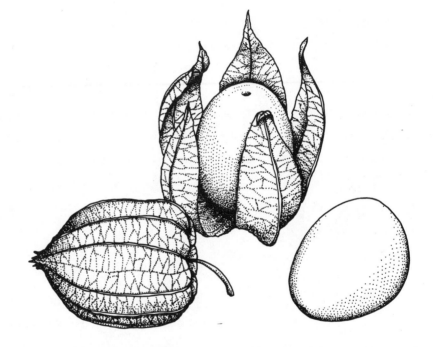

Its Latin name, *Physalis peruviana*, hints at its origins in the Andes region of Peru, but this relative of the husk tomato has also been cul-tivated outside of South America for hundreds of years. By the early 1800s, it was so popular in South Africa that it became known as cape gooseberry after the Cape of Good Hope, where it grew prolifically. In New Zealand, where it is a commercial crop, it is physallis, and else-where golden gooseberry, Chinese lantern, and strawberry tomato.

Charmingly concealed within a papery, lantern-shaped cape is a small, smooth, golden fruit, no more than three-eighths inch in di-ameter. Unlike other husk tomatoes which burst through their cover, the fruit is completely surrounded by the brownish coat which must be peeled back to get at the pleasantly tart-sweet berry.

CARAMBOLA

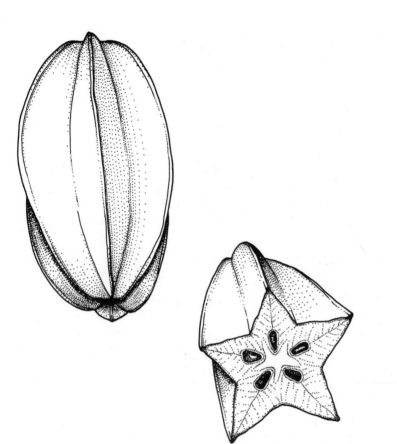

PEAK AVAILABILITY August to February.

SELECTION Choose firm, unblemished fruit with a golden color. The ribs turn brownish on their edges as the fruit ripens.

STORAGE Refrigerate ripe fruit in a plastic bag in crisper 3 to 4 days.

PREPARATION The peel is edible. Use whole, sliced, or mashed.

SERVING Eat the fruit whole, discarding the seeds, or slice crosswise and accompany with a wedge of lime. Use to garnish salads, poultry and meat dishes, or in fresh fruit desserts such as tarts, fruit plates, and sorbets. Prepare a tropical beverage by mashing the raw or cooked fruit, strain through a cheesecloth-lined sieve into a bowl to get juice, sweeten with sugar if needed, and serve over ice with a spring of mint.

NUTRITION Good source of vitamin A, vitamin C, and potassium.

Stubby, waxy, and yellow-green on the outside, with five prominent longitudinal ribs, the carambola (caram-BOH-la) is strikingly beautiful in cross section. When sliced it has an unusual, extremely decorative five-point star shape. Depending on where it is grown, the fruit is two to five inches long, and about two inches in diameter, with a translucent, juicy pulp that can be tart or tart-sweet. An Asian fruit, it is also cultivated in Florida where efforts are underway to develop less acidic, sweeter varieties.

Photograph: clockwise from upper left, coconut, red Cuban banana, passion fruit.

CHERIMOYA

PEAK AVAILABILITY November through May.

SELECTION Fruit ranges from ¼ pound to about 2½ pounds. A ripe cherimoya is a dull brownish-green, sometimes dotted with tan freckles, and is soft like a ripe peach. Avoid those with brown skins, an indication of overripeness.

STORAGE Ripen at room temperature; use immediately or refrigerate in a plastic bag in crisper 1 to 2 days.

PREPARATION To use pulp, scoop from skin and remove seeds.

SERVING Serve chilled halved or quartered, with a wedge of lime; use a spoon to scoop out the flesh, and discard the black seeds as you eat. Or use for fruit salads, sorbets, ice creams, cream pies, soufflés, and daiquiris.

NUTRITION Minor amounts of nutrients.

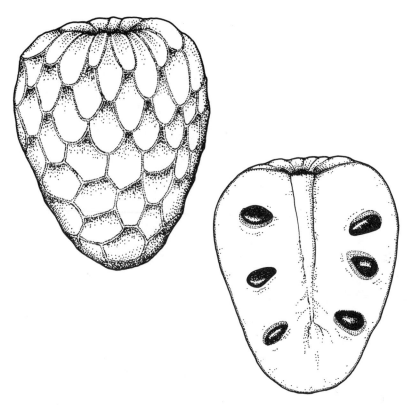

Mark Twain praised the cherimoya (chair-i-MOH-ya) as "deliciousness itself," so don't be put off by its reptilian exterior. Beneath the pale green, scaly skin is a creamy flesh that lusciously blends the flavors of papaya, pineapple, and banana, with a hint of pear. Because its custardlike consistency crystallizes when chilled, this South American fruit is also known as custard apple and sherbet fruit.

Although native to the highlands of Ecuador and Peru, cherimoyas have been grown in Southern California since before the turn of the century. They are costly even on the West Coast because cultivation is extremely labor intensive. Each female flower must be hand pollinated, and each fruit hand picked and sorted. Despite a high price tag, the demand for cherimoyas dramatically increases each year because of their exceptional flavor.

Photograph: cherimoya

COCONUT

The coconut is really a huge pit rather than a nut, the largest of the drupe fruits which also include apricots, dates, plums, cherries, and nectarines. The coconut palm is considered an essential crop in tropical regions because of its versatility and its long life. It will bear fruit six to ten years after germination and then continually for as long as eighty years. Every part of the tall, graceful tree is useful. The trunks provide timber for building; the leaves are woven into roofing, matting, baskets, and sun screens; from the seeds come food and fuel, as well as materials for soap, margarine, cooking oil, and cattle feed; the shells serve as eating utensils.

In the tropics coconut flesh is eaten at several stages of ripeness. The meat is firm and fully mature after a year, but at about seven months it is soft and sweet, like jelly. This "spoon coconut" is easily scooped from the shell and is bland enough to be fed to babies. When midripe the coconut liquid is at its sweetest and is enjoyed as a beverage. Contrary to common belief, this is called coconut water, not milk, the latter being the moisture extracted from the mature meat.

PEAK AVAILABILITY All year; most plentiful September through January.

SELECTION Choose fruit that is heavy for its size and filled with liquid. Shake the coconut; you should hear the liquid moving within. Avoid any with wet or moldy "eyes."

STORAGE In refrigerator crisper; unopened, it will keep for a month or longer.

PREPARATION To remove the coconut meat from the shell, pierce one or more of the eyes with an icepick; drain off the liquid. Place the drained coconut in a baking pan and bake in a 350° F. oven 15 to 20 minutes. Remove from the oven and tap with a hammer to crack open the shell; continue to hammer until cracked in several places. Remove the meat by inserting a sharp knife between meat and shell. Grate, a few chunks at a time with a little water, in a blender or food processor. To obtain coconut milk, soak the shredded coconut in an equal amount of hot water for up to an hour, then strain through a fine-meshed sieve, pressing as much liquid as possible out of the pulp; discard pulp. The extraction process can be repeated several times but the first pressing is the richest.

SERVING Use the shredded coconut in baked goods, desserts, and as a condiment for curries. The Hawaiians use coconut milk to make *haupia*, a stiff cornstarch pudding served in cubes. Coconut milk is also part of savory chicken and fish dishes. Add the coconut milk to curries, ice creams, and beverages.

NUTRITION Coconut meat is a good source of iron.

FEIJOA

PEAK AVAILABILITY March through June for New Zealand varieties; September through December for California fruit.

SELECTION Ripe fruit will yield to gentle pressure and give off an enticing perfume.

STORAGE Refrigerate ripe fruit in a plastic bag in crisper, or ripen at room temperature and then refrigerate and use as soon as possible.

PREPARATION The flesh darkens when exposed to air; to maintain the natural color, coat the sliced surface with lemon or lime juice. Peel before eating raw or cooking, unless eating halved from the shell.

SERVING Halve and eat scooped fresh from the shell, sprinkled with lemon or lime juice. Serve as an appetizer with sliced meats or fish, such as prosciutto or smoked salmon. Add to a salad or fruit plate (if you are growing feijoa shrubs in your garden, the flower petals are edible; sprinkle on salads as a garnish). Use for preserves and jellies. Sauté fruit halves in butter with ginger and lime juice as an accompaniment for roast pork, ham, or poultry. Puree and use in a sorbet or mousse.

NUTRITION Good source of vitamin C.

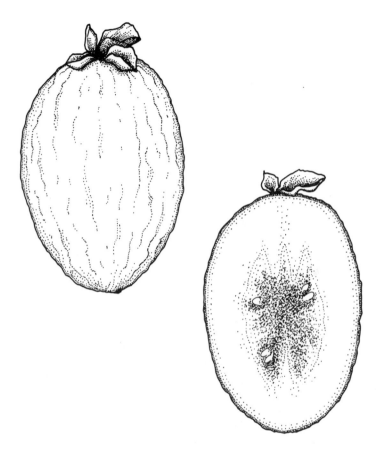

Juicy, sweet, and extremely aromatic, feijoas (fee-HO-as or fee-JO-as) have become a major commercial crop in New Zealand, where they are also prized by home gardeners for their interesting foliage and beautiful red-tufted white flowers. Actually, this gray-green, smooth-skinned oval fruit is native to South America, and is now grown throughout the South Pacific and in California.

Its flavor is a refreshing blend of pineapple, pear, and banana, with a hint of guava, which perhaps inspired its other name, pineapple guava. Its flesh is creamy-white and slightly granular like that of a pear, with several tiny, edible seeds contained in its jellylike center. Most varieties are egg-shaped and about three inches long.

FRAISE DES BOIS

PEAK AVAILABILITY May through August.

SELECTION Choose fresh-looking berries with a bright color.

STORAGE Like all berries, these are sold in baskets. Refrigerate un-washed and loosely covered in bas-ket in crisper up to 3 days.

PREPARATION Rinse gently in a bowl of cold water.

SERVING Presentation should show-case the berry's full flavor. Serve simply in a bowl with crème fraîche, or with a splash of fruit-flavored li-queur and a spoonful of whipped cream. Use to top tarts or cream puffs, or as the base for sorbet or ice cream—an unforgettable dessert.

NUTRITION Good source of vitamin C.

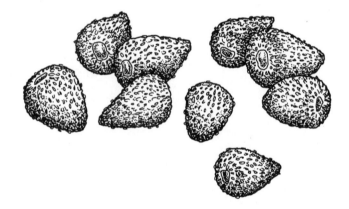

This tiny wild strawberry is considered a delicacy throughout the European continent, particularly in France and Italy. It has begun to appear in this country to a limited degree in specialty produce markets and in home gardens. "Strawberries of the woods" have an exquisite, intense flavor—sweet and highly perfumed—relative to their petite size and are wonderful for liqueurs. Scarce and fragile, fraises des bois (fres-day-BWAH) are priced in the luxury class when available.

GOOSEBERRY

PEAK AVAILABILITY May through August. New Zealand berries are in season October through December.

SELECTION Choose firm, fresh berries.

STORAGE Fresh berries will keep at room temperature or in a plastic bag in refrigerator crisper 1 to 2 days.

PREPARATION Remove tops and tails (easily done with scissors).

SERVING Use tart fruit in pies, savory or dessert sauces, cobblers, and crisps. Prepare in a fool: Crush cooked and sweetened berries and mix with whipped cream or custard. Serve spiced berries as a condiment.

NUTRITION Good source of vitamin C, fiber, and potassium, and a fair source of vitamin A.

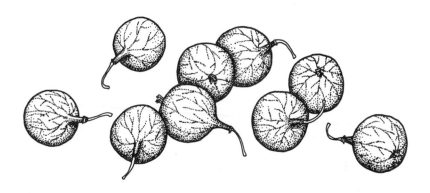

Gooseberries have been grown since the eleventh century in England, where they are traditional pie fruits, used for jams, jellies, and sauces, and as a fresh dessert. They have held a place of honor in gardens there since the time of Henry VIII, and perhaps reached their peak of popularity in the 1800s when gooseberry clubs were widely established to promote the berry's cultivation and improvement. The fruit is also eaten in continental Europe, but not to the same extent as in England. The name gooseberry is derived from the German word *krausbeere*, meaning "curly berry."

Despite attempts by colonists, the European fruit did not flourish in the New World, as it was susceptible to a native mildew. Indigenous American varieties were not considered as sweet and flavorful and were found to be carriers of a white pine blight; their culture was eventually curtailed, by state law in some cases. A hybrid of the English and American strain was developed, and the fruit is now harvested commercially on a small scale in Oregon, Washington, and Michigan. Imports are also coming in from New Zealand.

The berries are related to currants and look like small, striped grapes with smooth or fuzzy skins. Ripe berries can be green, pink, yellow, or white; all varieties are green and tart when immature, and are best for cooking at this stage.

GUAVA

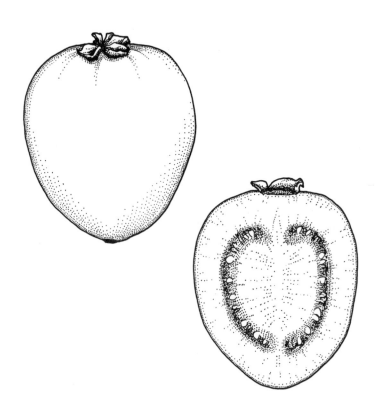

PEAK AVAILABILITY September through January for California fruits; March through June for the New Zealand crop.

SELECTION Select firm, fresh fruit; avoid dry, shriveled, or dull ones.

STORAGE Let ripen until fruit yields to gentle pressure and aroma is very noticeable. Refrigerate for up to two weeks.

PREPARATION To eat raw: wash and trim away stem and blossom ends. Thinly peel fruit before pureeing.

SERVING Halve and eat raw from shell when very ripe and sweet. Use somewhat firm fruit for jams, jellies, and condiments (the fruit is high in pectin). Puree for sauce, sorbet, ice cream, or mousse. Or cook down into a paste, cut in cubes, and eat as a confection. The juice can be a beverage by itself or added to other drinks.

NUTRITION Excellent source of vitamin C and vitamin A.

Guavas are native to South America, but have spread throughout the world's tropical and subtropical regions. In this country, they are grown in California, Florida, and Hawaii where they proliferate like weeds. The fruit can be oval to round, is about two to three inches long, and has a thin green, yellow, red, purple, or even black skin. Depending on type, the flesh ranges from white to yellow to coral to shocking pink, with edible seeds, a distinctive tart to sweet flavor, and a pleasant scent.

   All varieties are highly nutritious. They are one of the best sources of vitamin C—less than one cup of fresh juice will fulfill an adult's daily dietary requirement. Some varieties even surpass citrus fruits in their concentration of this nutrient. The pinker-fleshed ones supply vitamin A as well.

KIWIFRUIT

PEAK AVAILABILITY November through April for California fruits; May through October for New Zealand varieties.

SELECTION The fruit is marketed firm. Ripen at room temperature in a sealed plastic bag along with an apple or banana. When ripe it will yield easily under gentle pressure. Avoid those that are overly soft or bruised.

STORAGE Refrigerate ripe fruit in a plastic bag in crisper 1 to 2 weeks.

PREPARATION Pare with a knife before eating raw or cooking.

SERVING Halve, sprinkle with lime juice, and eat with a spoon. Peel, slice crosswise, and use in a fruit or main-course salad, or as a topping for a tart or a frozen dessert. Puree and use as a sauce, or as the base for a sorbet. In Australia and New Zealand kiwis are used for pavlova, a meringue dessert (page 123).

NUTRITION Excellent source of vitamin C (almost twice that of an orange) and a good source of potassium.

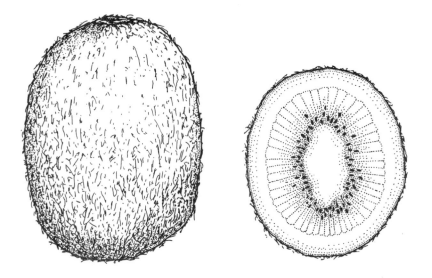

Before it was kiwifruit, it was the Chinese gooseberry, the fruit of a vine which originated in Asia and was introduced into New Zealand in the early part of this century for the ornamental plant market. When growers decided to export the fruit in the late 1950s, they felt its name should be changed to avoid confusion with the green gooseberry and to create a strong identification with their island nation. They named it kiwifruit, after New Zealand's famous flightless native bird.

Since then, the kiwi has experienced phenomenal success as a marketed fruit and has stimulated the cultivation and export of many other subtropical fruits. The United States Department of Agriculture encouraged California farmers to grow kiwifruit almost fifty years ago. That state has become the major American supplier, with a growing season that complements New Zealand's, making kiwis an all-year commodity.

The fruit is shaped and sized like a lime, with a nondescript, fuzzy brown skin. But beneath this unassuming cover hides a dazzling emerald-green flesh, dotted with a ring of tiny, crunchy black seeds that surround a creamy yellow core. Its tropical flavor has been compared to many fruits, but most often described as a juicy, tart-sweet blend of strawberry, melon, and banana.

KUMQUAT

PEAK AVAILABILITY November through February from California and Florida.

SELECTION Choose firm, glossy, bright fruit.

STORAGE In a plastic bag in refrigerator crisper, uncut, a month or more.

PREPARATION For fresh salads, wash, dry, slice thinly, and seed. Other preparation depends on the recipe.

SERVING Slice and include in fruit or vegetable main-dish salads. Use for preserves, jams, marmalades, and condiments. Serve cooked as an accompaniment to duck, pork, turkey, or fish.

NUTRITION Good source of vitamin C, potassium, and fiber, and a fair source of vitamin A and calcium.

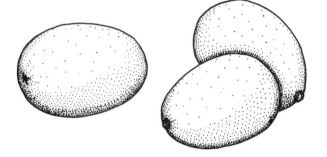

The Chinese named this tiny oval citrus cousin "golden orange." Less than an inch long, it appears to be a miniature of that fruit. Unlike the orange, however, the kumquat's edible skin is sweeter than its flesh which can be quite tart and pungent, a characteristic echoed in its gingery aroma. In the Orient, where kumquats have been eaten for thousands of years, they are a symbol of good luck. Most often they are pickled or preserved, rather than eaten raw.

LITCHI

PEAK AVAILABILITY June and July.

SELECTION Skin should look fresh, not withered.

STORAGE Unshelled in a plastic bag in refrigerator crisper; use as soon as possible.

PREPARATION Peel and pit.

SERVING Enjoy shelled out of hand. Or use in a fruit salad, as a dessert, or as a garnish.

NUTRITION Good source of vitamin C.

Asians have enjoyed the sweet, slightly acid litchi (LEE-chee) for over two thousand years. It was so prized in China that a T'ang Dynasty emperor was said to have organized relays of horsemen to deliver daily supplies to his concubine.

If you've only eaten the seeded, canned variety offered as a standard dessert in many Chinese restaurants, you probably wouldn't recognize the fresh litchi at the market. The snow-white fruits, which have the consistency of grapes, are encased in a coarse, leathery, red shell, about the size of a large strawberry. Within the translucent, firm flesh is a brown seed. Dried litchis are like raisins and are called litchi nuts.

Domestically litchis are grown in California, Florida, and Hawaii on evergreen trees that can reach forty feet in height. Imports are shipped to us from Mexico and Asia. Other common spellings include lychee, litchee, and leechee.

LONGAN

PEAK AVAILABILITY July and August.

SELECTION The shell should be intact and the flesh unblemished.

STORAGE Unshelled in a plastic bag in refrigerator crisper; use as soon as possible.

PREPARATION Shell when ready to use.

SERVING Use the fresh fruit in salads and desserts.

NUTRITION Good source of vitamin C, iron, and phosphorus.

Longans are round, juicy, gelatinous fruits that are similar to litchis, but with a smooth, yellow-brown shell, rather than a warty red one. Although they have a slightly different flavor described as sweet-salty, they are used interchangeably with litchis. Like that fruit longans develop in clusters and are natives of tropical Asia. They are also called dragon's eye.

The fruit comes to market from Hawaii and the Dominican Republic, and grows well in southern Florida.

LOQUAT

PEAK AVAILABILITY March through May.

SELECTION Choose firm, unblemished fruit.

STORAGE Ripen at room temperature; refrigerate ripe fruit in a plastic bag in crisper 2 to 3 days.

PREPARATION Peel.

SERVING Slice or dice the peeled fruit and use in fruit salads or compotes. Bake slices with roast pork. Use like kumquats in chutneys, jams, and jellies. Puree and use as a sauce.

NUTRITION Good source of vitamin A and potassium.

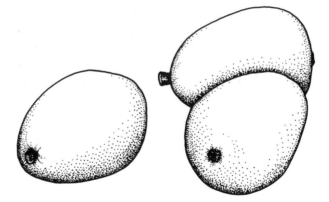

The loquat's appearance makes it hard to understand why it and the apple are in the same botanical family. Loquats are small, pear-shaped, and yellow, about one-and-one-half to three inches in diameter. The juicy pulp is white, yellow, or deep orange, with several large black seeds and a tart-sweet flavor which sweetens as the fruit ripens.

Loquats have long been popular in China, Japan, northern India, and around the Mediterranean. In California, Florida, and the Gulf states this evergreen tree is planted for its beauty as well as its fruit.

MANGO

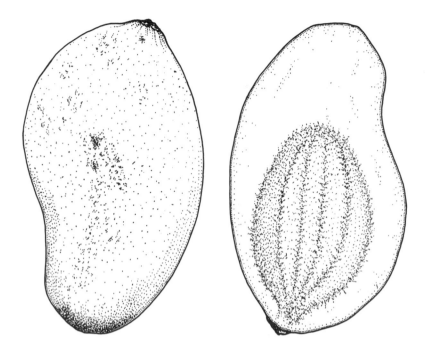

A Victorian writer praised the mango as "incomparably superior to any fruit the earth can produce." Few who have tasted one at its peak of ripeness would consider this description a flowery exaggeration. The British probably first tried mangoes in India, where it is thought to have originated and where it is a favorite fruit. The mango tree, which can grow forty to fifty feet high with widespreading branches, is sacred to the Hindus. Traders and travelers introduced the tree to tropical areas in other parts of the world where it has become as common as the apple is in temperate regions.

The fruit varies in shape, color, and texture depending on type, of which there are many. In our markets mangoes are usually round to oval with a skin that is either green mottled with red or green-yellow with a rose blush. As the fruit ripens, its warm coloration increases. The best varieties have a juicy, firm, golden-orange flesh, without the stringiness that makes some types objectionable. To be eaten fresh mangoes must be perfectly ripe to display their unique flavor which resembles a peach with overtones of papaya, apricot, and pineapple. Eaten immature, they can taste like turpentine.

PEAK AVAILABILITY Most plentiful May through August, and sporadically throughout the year. Grown in Florida, Haiti, Brazil, and Mexico.

SELECTION Skin color varies with the variety. Most come to the market not fully ripe; very green or ultra-hard ones have been picked prematurely and will never ripen.

STORAGE Ripen at room temperature in a paper bag pierced with a few holes until the fruit yields to gentle pressure and the color heightens. Refrigerate ripe fruit in a plastic bag in crisper and eat as soon as possible.

PREPARATION Mangoes are messy to eat and hard to peel and seed, but worth the fuss. There are two ways to get to the fruit: Score the thin, tough skin in four sections and peel the skin back like a banana; slice the fruit away from the flat, elliptical seed. The second method is to slice the fruit (with skin) from the flat sides of the seed and then as best you can from the narrow edges. Score the flesh into ½-inch cubes and peel by cutting under flesh with a curved paring knife or grapefruit knife, or scoop from the skin with a spoon.

SERVING A ripe mango needs nothing more than a squeeze of lime to enhance its flavor. If desired, add the ripe fruit to sweet and savory salads, pies, cakes, sorbets, ice cream, mousses, and beverages. When green and hard, mangoes are a main ingredient in chutneys and preserves.

NUTRITION Excellent source of vitamin A, and fair source of vitamin C and potassium.

PEAK AVAILABILITY May through November, but increasingly in markets all year.

SELECTION Look for smooth, unblemished fruit, at least half yellow; avoid green, hard ones or any with bruises. If just tinged with yellow, allow 5 to 7 days at room temperature to ripen.

STORAGE In a plastic bag in refrigerator crisper 1 to 2 days.

PREPARATION To eat fresh: halve or quarter, and remove seeds, if desired. To cube or puree: peel first.

SERVING Use like a melon. Papayas are wonderful served alone with fresh lemon or lime juice, or stuffed with strawberries or raspberries. Or, fill a papaya half with chicken or shrimp salad. Cut up for salads. Sauté or bake with ginger and lime as a meat accompaniment. Puree for a sorbet, mousse, ice cream, or beverage. Grind the seeds and add to salad dressings or meat marinades. Use green papayas like summer squash, and also as part of chutneys, pickles, and relishes.

NUTRITION Excellent source of vitamin C and vitamin A.

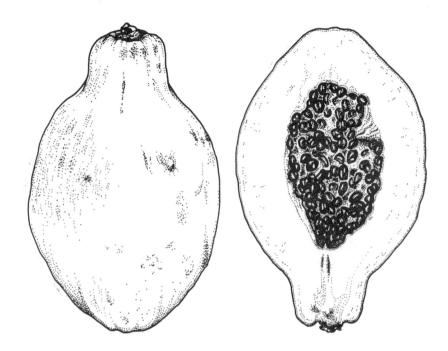

In contrast to the coconut palm, which is productive for decades, the tropical papaya tree peaks after only two or three years and is cut down. As if to make up for its brief life span, it explodes from seed to mature, fruit-bearing tree in as little as seven months, and then fruits prolifically until its decline.

Usually two varieties appear in American markets. Most familiar is the Solo from Hawaii, a pear-shaped fruit about six inches long and three to four inches in diameter, averaging about two pounds. The larger Mexican papaya is quite elongated—often ten to twenty inches from end to end—and can weigh as much as ten pounds. Papaya skin is thick, smooth, and slightly ridged. It is green when immature, ripening to greenish-yellow or deep gold depending on variety. The flesh ranges from pastel orange to a rich salmon, with a juicy, soft, yet melonlike texture. In the center cavity are tiny, shiny, black edible seeds which are considered a digestive aid, but are usually discarded. Both the fruit, especially when green, and the leaves contain papain, an enzyme that breaks down protein and is used in meat tenderizers.

PASSION FRUIT

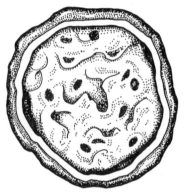

PEAK AVAILABILITY Late February to early October.

SELECTION A shriveled shell is the key to ripeness.

STORAGE Ripen at room temperature until the skin wrinkles, then refrigerate in a plastic bag in crisper 2 to 3 days.

PREPARATION To eat fresh, cut fruit in half and eat from the shell, including the many small black seeds which are so firmly embedded in the pulp that they are impossible to pick out. Squeezing the pulp through a sieve or several layers of cheesecloth will produce juice free of seeds.

SERVING Serve on the half shell with a squeeze of lime or lemon juice. Puree the pulp until the seeds are ground like pepper (or sieve out the seeds) and then incorporate in sauces, pies, sorbets, mousses, bombes, and ice creams. Blend with other fruit juices for a refreshing punch. Freeze the fruit and eat partially thawed.

NUTRITION Good source of vitamin A and vitamin C.

Passion fruit was named by the Spanish, who supposedly thought the markings of its flowers resembled the symbols of the Crucifixion. The flowers of the *Passiflora edulis* vine are spectacular and showy, unlike the fruit that develop from it. When fully mature, the fruit's formerly smooth green skin becomes brittle and wrinkled and darkens to a deep brownish-purple—far from a tropical beauty. But unlike the wizened shell, the aromatic, yellow-orange pulp contained within is sweet and appealing.

More acidic, yellow-skinned varieties also exist which are about the same size and shape as the purple fruits—oval and about three inches long. The giant granadilla is another species of *Passiflora*, with fruits almost four times longer than the purple passion fruit, and growing up to six pounds. Passion fruit is native to Brazil, and is now grown in New Zealand, Australia, Africa, Hawaii, Florida, and California.

PEPINO

PEAK AVAILABILITY August to December for the California crop; February to June for New Zealand imports.

SELECTION The skin of ripe fruit will turn from green to yellow.

STORAGE Ripen at room temperature until fruit yellows and yields to gentle pressure. Refrigerate ripe fruit in a plastic bag in crisper 2 to 3 days.

PREPARATION Halve and scoop out seeds.

SERVING Eat on the half shell sprinkled with lemon or lime juice. Peel and serve fresh in fruit salads, or cooked in compotes and chutneys. Slice and sauté in butter with ginger and lime juice to serve with grilled chicken, fish, or lamb. Puree for a sorbet.

NUTRITION Good source of vitamin C.

Although used as a fruit, the pepino grows on a bushy plant grouped in the same nightshade family as the eggplant, tomato, and potato. Its skin is distinctively marked—yellow striped with lavender to deep purple. The flavor of the pale greenish-yellow to yellow flesh suggests an unusual blend of cantaloupe, honeydew melon, and pear, scented with cucumber. Also known as the melon pear, the pepino originated in the Andes in South America and is grown commercially in New Zealand and California.

PERSIMMON

This decorative orange fruit adds brilliant color to the autumn market scene and to holiday tables. Known as the "apple of the Orient" because the most common species (*Diospyros kaki*) originated there, it is popularly available in two varieties. One, the Hachiya, has a slightly pointed oval shape. The Fuyu is flatter, much like a tomato, with a slightly crisp texture when ripe. Another species is native to North America and grows wild in the eastern states. It is smaller and much more astringent than the *kaki*.

Probably, a bite of an unripe wild persimmon prompted Captain John Smith of Jamestown to write of this fruit that "if it not be ripe, it will draw a man's mouth awrie with torment." At their peak of flavor persimmons are luscious and sweet. Eaten before they are ready, they are uncomfortably puckery and chalky.

POMEGRANATE

PEAK AVAILABILITY October through November.

SELECTION Choose fresh-looking fruit heavy for its size with good color. Generally, the larger the fruit, the juicier the flesh.

STORAGE Keep in a fruit bowl for several days, or until the fruit begins to dry and shrivel. Use immediately (do not let the skin harden or it will be difficult to peel). To keep longer, store in a plastic bag in refrigerator crisper 1 week.

PREPARATION To get at the seeds, break apart the fruit with your hands and also by hand, pick out the seeds from each section. To extract the juice, cut the fruit in half and ream with a juice extractor. Handling and eating an opened pomegranate is very messy. Be aware that the juice stains.

SERVING Use the seeds in salads, stews, soups, poultry stuffings, or scatter them over a fruit compote or dessert. The juice is a wonderful marinade for lamb, pork, or poultry.

NUTRITION Fair source of potassium.

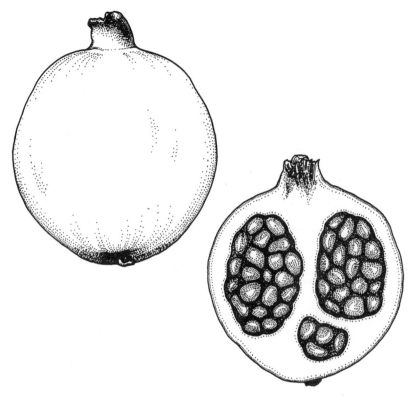

When the children of Israel dreamed of the Promised Land, they envisioned a "land of wheat, and barley, and vines, and fig trees, and pomegranates." This exotic scarlet fruit, native to Persia, played a role in the religious rites and mythology of many peoples. Because of its profusion of seeds, the ancients connected it with procreation and abundance, and believed that Aphrodite, goddess of love, planted it on the island of Cyprus. Today, the pomegranate is grown widely in Asia, around the Mediterranean, and to a smaller extent in California.

This fruit's botanical name in part means "apple of many seeds," referring to its shape and the profusion of little seeds contained within the bitter white membrane that divides the interior. Each seed is surrounded by juicy red pulp, which is messy and difficult to extract, but its tart sweetness rewards the persistent. Pomegranate juice is the principal ingredient in grenadine syrup.

PRICKLY PEAR

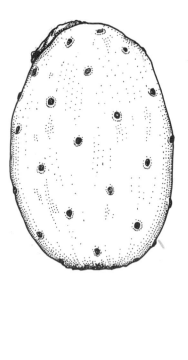
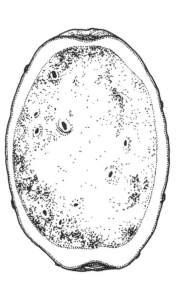

PEAK AVAILABILITY September through December.

SELECTION Choose firm but not hard fruit with a shiny appearance.

STORAGE At room temperature for a few days, then refrigerate in a plastic bag in crisper 2 to 3 days.

PREPARATION If any sharp spines remain, remove with pliers. To peel: cut off a small slice from both ends of fruit; slit skin from top to bottom and peel back. To remove the hard seeds: press through a sieve or food mill.

SERVING Eat the fruit peeled and sliced with fresh lemon or lime juice. Cube and use in a baked fruit crisp. Candy and use in fruit cakes. Puree and use for sorbets, ice creams, and dessert sauces. The juice can be reduced to a syrup for pancakes and desserts.

NUTRITION Good source of fiber, and a fair source of vitamin C and calcium.

The prickly pear is an edible cactus that also produces a thorny, round- to pear-shaped fruit, which is yellow to crimson (depending on the source) with sweet, light pink to magenta flesh. The fruit is variously known as tuna, Indian fig, barbary fig, and cactus pear. This is another of those plants native to the New World—Mexico in this case—that the early explorers carried to Spain and then on to the many subtropical areas where it now grows.

The prickly pear was a favorite of North American Indians, who dried the fruit and pressed it into thin cakes which stored and transported well. They also combined it with nuts and dried meats to make an energy-rich patty considered a tonic for sluggish winter digestions.

Although the fruit grows with sharp spines on its skin, they are usually removed before it gets to market. In Mexico street vendors and markets sell peeled prickly pears as a snack.

QUINCE

PEAK AVAILABILITY September through December.

SELECTION Choose large golden fruit. Some blemishes may appear on the skin but are not a sign of poor quality.

STORAGE At cool room temperature for a week, or in a plastic bag in refrigerator crisper for months.

PREPARATION Remove core. Fruit can be cooked with or without skin.

SERVING Bake whole, peeled quinces, or cut up and add to stews, or poach and serve with meat. Traditionally incorporated into preserves, jams, and jellies, and in dishes with apples and pears.

NUTRITION A fair source of vitamin C.

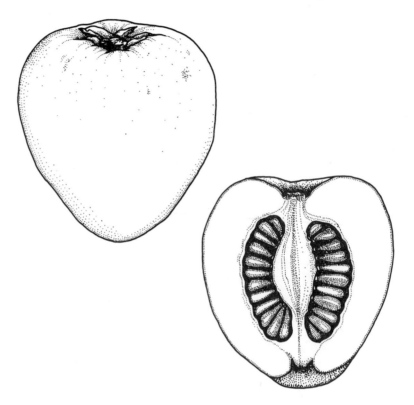

To the Greeks and Romans, the fragrant quince symbolized love and fertility. The gift of this fruit to a loved one was tantamount to a marriage proposal. The small quince tree is native to western Asia, where it has flourished for thousands of years, appreciated for its beautiful white and pink blossoms as well as its fruit. A quince resembles a lumpy, wooly pear, with greenish skin that ripens to a rich yellow. Its hard flesh varies from creamy white to apricot, and is so tart and astringent, even when ripe, that it is never eaten raw.

With its overbearing tang and high pectin content the quince is ideal for jams, jellies, and other preserves. When cooked with sugar, its flavor mellows and the liquid deepens to an autumnal pink-amber hue. The word *marmalade* comes from *marmelo*, "quince" in Portuguese.

RED BARTLETT PEAR

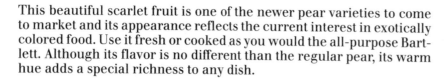

PEAK AVAILABILITY August through
October.

SELECTION Choose unblemished,
well-shaped fruit.

STORAGE Like all pears, the fruit is
picked underripe. Let ripen in a
pierced paper bag until it yields to
gentle pressure. Refrigerate ripe
fruit in a plastic bag in crisper 2 to 3
days.

PREPARATION Core, and pare if the
recipe requires.

SERVING Pears marry well with
spices, citrus flavors, chocolate,
nuts, and cheeses. Slice and add to
green salads with toasted walnuts,
hazelnuts, or pecans. Poach and
serve with ice cream and chocolate
sauce. Bake in pies, tortes, and
crumbles.

NUTRITION Minor amounts of nutrients.

This beautiful scarlet fruit is one of the newer pear varieties to come
to market and its appearance reflects the current interest in exotically
colored food. Use it fresh or cooked as you would the all-purpose Bartlett. Although its flavor is no different than the regular pear, its warm
hue adds a special richness to any dish.

RED CUBAN BANANA

PEAK AVAILABILITY Sporadically all year.

SELECTION When ripe, the fruit feels soft, the skin darkens, and has black speckles.

STORAGE Ripen at room temperature and eat as soon as possible.

PREPARATION Remove skin.

SERVING As a breakfast fruit, slice and top with walnuts and cream. Use in any recipe that calls for bananas.

NUTRITION Good source of vitamin A and potassium.

A purplish-red skin wraps up the sweet, creamy flesh of these short, fat bananas, one of several uncommon varieties showing up in specialty produce markets now. Their flavor and color are slightly more intense than that of yellow bananas and their cost is a lot more. They come to this country from Ecuador, but also grow in Hawaii.

RHUBARB

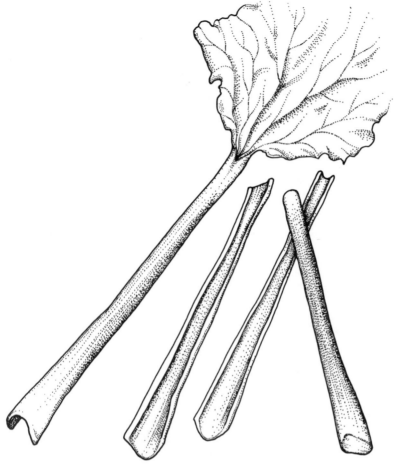

PEAK AVAILABILITY Late spring, but stretching from January through June.

SELECTION Choose crisp, bright-hued, medium-thick stalks with fresh green leaves. Hothouse rhubarb has paler stalks; field rhubarb's stalks are a deeper red.

STORAGE In a plastic bag in refrigerator crisper 1 to 2 days.

PREPARATION Trim away leaves and discard. Trim stalks at ends and cut stalks into ½- to 3-inch pieces. Rhubarb requires both sweetening and cooking.

SERVING Serve as a sauce over ice cream or custard. Use in a cold soup, mousse, or ice cream. Add to applesauce. Combine with strawberries in a pie, tart, cobbler, or fool.

NUTRITION Fair source of vitamin A and potassium.

Botanically rhubarb is a vegetable, but it falls in the category of a fruit because of the way we use it. Traditionally it appears in tarts, cobblers, crumbles, and fools, especially in combination with strawberries. Rhubarb is one of those homey, country foods tied to our rural past that are becoming increasingly popular with young chefs as they examine and attempt to update American regional cooking.

Only the pinkish-to-red stalks are used. The green leaves have such a high concentration of oxalic acid that they can be toxic if eaten. Commercially rhubarb is grown in Washington, California, and Michigan.

SAPOTE

PEAK AVAILABILITY May through November.

SELECTION Choose firm, blemish-free fruit.

STORAGE Ripen at room temperature; refrigerate in a plastic bag in crisper 1 to 2 days.

PREPARATION Peel and slice; remove elliptical seeds.

SERVING Eat fresh, out of hand. Peel, slice, and seed, then drizzle with lemon or lime juice to keep from darkening and use in fruit salads. Puree with a little orange zest or vanilla extract for a sorbet, ice cream, or mousse.

NUTRITION Fair source of vitamin A and vitamin C.

This Mexican native, pronounced sah-POH-tay, looks like a green or greenish-yellow apple with a slightly pointed, rather than indented, bottom. It grows in Florida and Southern California as well as Central America. The fruit's sweet, cream-colored pulp is custardy like a cherimoya—both are called custard apple—and tastes like a blend of peach and banana. Less common is the dark-fleshed black sapote.

TAMARILLO

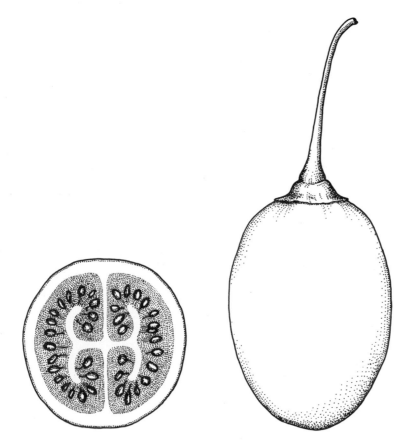

Perhaps to establish it clearly as a fruit in the world market, the name of this subtropical plant was changed by New Zealand exporters from tree tomato to tamarillo. Two types of tamarillos are grown commercially in that country: one is brilliant red with an astringent, sweet-sour orange flesh and dark seeds; the other is golden with a sweeter yellow flesh and pale seeds. Both are shaped like a pointed plum with a small green cap and long, dark-green stem. The unique flavor is hard to describe—something like a cross between a plum and a tomato. In New Zealand the tamarillo is known as a "vegefruit," and is always eaten cooked. The satiny skin is peeled and discarded as it is very bitter.

Photograph: prickly pear

Overleaf: clockwise from upper right, chanterelle, cultivated oyster, an uncommon variety of cultivated oyster, wild oyster, enoki, shiitake.

the new
HARVEST
recipes

APPETIZERS & FIRST COURSES

CALIFORNIA-STYLE CALZONE

Whole Wheat Pizza Crust
  (follows)
4 mild Italian sausages
1 large red onion, chopped
2 zucchini or golden zucchini,
  thinly sliced
2 tablespoons olive oil
½ pound mushrooms, sliced
1 sweet red bell pepper, cored,
  seeded, and chopped
1 tablespoon chopped fresh basil
Freshly ground black pepper
8 ounces mozzarella cheese,
  shredded
4 ounces Monterey Jack cheese,
  shredded
4 ounces freshly grated Parmesan or Romano cheese

Prepare dough for Whole Wheat Pizza Crust. Place sausages in a medium saucepan; cover with water and bring to a boil. Remove from heat and let stand 15 minutes; drain and slice.

In a large skillet sauté onion and zucchini in 1 tablespoon oil until limp. Add mushrooms and red pepper and sauté 1 minute longer. Remove from heat and mix in basil and pepper; let cool a few minutes. Mix in mozzarella, Jack, and half the Parmesan cheese

Divide dough in half. Roll out one half on a floured surface to a 14-inch circle. Place on a lightly greased pizza pan or baking sheet. Cover half of the dough with half of the filling. Fold dough over to cover filling; pinch edges to seal. Repeat with remaining dough and filling for second calzone. Bake in a 425° F. oven 10 minutes. Reduce heat to 375° F. and bake 20 to 25 minutes longer, or until crust is golden brown. Remove from oven and brush top of dough with remaining olive oil and sprinkle with reserved Parmesan cheese. Serve hot. Each calzone makes 2 to 4 servings, depending on appetites.

WHOLE WHEAT PIZZA CRUST In a medium bowl place 1½ cups warm water (105° F.). Sprinkle 1 package active dry yeast into water. Let stand until yeast has dissolved, about 5 minutes. Stir in 1 teaspoon *each* salt and sugar, 1 tablespoon olive oil, and ¾ cup *each* unbleached flour and whole wheat flour. Add additional flour to make a soft dough. Knead with the dough hook of a heavy duty electric mixer or turn out onto a floured surface and knead lightly by hand about 10 minutes, or until dough is smooth and satiny. Place dough in a bowl, cover, and let rise 45 minutes, or until doubled in bulk.

DRIED TOMATO AND EGGPLANT PIZZA

1 medium Chinese eggplant
Salt
4 tablespoons olive oil
1 red onion, thinly sliced
3 cloves garlic, pressed
Whole Wheat Pizza Crust (page 74)
⅔ cup dried tomatoes (page 116)
¼ cup oil from tomatoes
½ pound mozzarella cheese, shredded
3 tablespoons grated dry Jack or Romano cheese
2 tablespoons minced fresh basil or cilantro for garnish

Slice eggplant ¼ inch thick; sprinkle with salt. Drain in a colander 30 minutes. Rinse well and pat dry. Sauté in 2 tablespoons olive oil until golden. Remove eggplant. Sauté onion and garlic in remaining oil until limp.
   For Whole Wheat Pizza Crust: Roll out dough on a floured surface to a 14-inch circle. Place in lightly-greased pizza pan. In a food processor or blender puree tomatoes with tomato oil; spread over dough. Cover with eggplant and onion; sprinkle with cheese. Bake in a 450° F. oven 15 minutes, or until golden brown. Remove from oven and garnish with minced basil or cilantro. Makes 8 appetizer servings.

WHOLE WHEAT CREPES WITH DRIED TOMATOES AND CHEVRE

¾ cup milk
2 eggs
½ cup whole wheat flour
About 2 tablespoons butter
4 ounces chèvre or natural cream cheese
1 dozen dried tomato halves, packed in oil and drained (page 116)
Fresh cilantro or basil for garnish

For crêpes: In a blender or food processor blend the milk, eggs, and flour until smooth. Let stand 10 to 15 minutes. Heat a 6-inch crêpe pan over medium heat; add ½ teaspoon butter and tilt pan to coat surface. Pour in just enough batter to coat surface (barely 2 tablespoons) and quickly tilt pan to cover surface. Cook until golden brown on the edges and dry on top, about 1 minute. Turn out onto a plate. (It is not necessary to cook both sides.) Stack crêpes.
   To assemble: Line a large baking sheet with foil and lightly butter. Place half the crêpes on the foil without overlapping, spread each with chèvre and cover with tomato halves. Top each with another crêpe. Bake in a 400° F. oven 5 minutes, or just until hot through. Garnish each serving with a sprig or two of cilantro or basil. Serve whole. Makes 4 first-course servings.

DRIED TOMATO-CHEESE TORTA

¾ pound unsalted butter, softened
8 ounces natural cream cheese, softened
4 ounces goat cheese or natural cream cheese, softened
¾ cup dried tomatoes (page 116)
2 tablespoons oil from tomatoes
Cilantro and dried tomatoes for garnish
Crackers or crudités for accompaniment

Line a decorative or conical 1-quart mold with a double layer of well-rinsed cheesecloth. In a medium bowl beat butter and cheeses until creamy. In a food processor puree tomatoes and oil. In cheesecloth-lined mold layer cheese mixture and tomato filling (make three cheese and two tomato layers, beginning and ending with cheese); do not use too much filling or it will ooze out. Fold over cheesecloth and seal mold with plastic wrap; refrigerate overnight. To serve, unmold, remove cheesecloth, and garnish with cilantro and dried tomatoes. Serve with crackers or crudités. Makes about 16 appetizer servings.

TOMATILLO CON QUESO

6 fresh tomatillos, husked and
 chopped
1 medium onion, chopped
2 tablespoons butter
1 tomato, peeled, seeded, and
 chopped
2 chopped green chilies
2 tablespoons chopped fresh
 cilantro
¾ pound teleme or Cheddar
 cheese, sliced
Small hot fried tortillas or tortilla
 chips

In a medium saucepan simmer
tomatillos in a small amount of
water until soft, about 15 minutes. In a large skillet sauté
onion in butter until soft, about 5
minutes. Add tomatillos, tomato,
chilies, and cilantro. Simmer
gently 10 minutes, uncovered.
Add cheese and heat over low
heat until melted. Serve with tortillas. Makes 10 to 12 appetizer
servings.

GARDEN VEGETABLES WITH PISTACHIO AIOLI

Aioli:
1 egg
2 tablespoons white wine
 vinegar
1 tablespoon fresh lemon juice
½ teaspoon salt
½ teaspoon Dijon-style mustard
4 to 5 cloves garlic, peeled
½ cup *each* olive oil and safflower oil
⅓ cup chopped pistachios or
 toasted pine nuts*

Fennel bulb, trimmed and
 quartered
Snow peas (left whole), strings
 removed
Baby carrots, peeled
Cauliflower, cut into flowerets
Radishes (with tops), washed
Baby asparagus spears, trimmed
Young fava beans, left in the pod
Green, gold, or red bell peppers,
 cored, seeded, and cut in
 strips
Mushrooms (left whole),
 trimmed
Yellow or red plum tomatoes,
 halved
Peeled and sliced jícama

For Aioli Sauce: In a food processor or blender blend the egg, vinegar, lemon juice, salt, mustard,
and garlic until smooth. With
motor running, gradually pour
in oil in a fine, steady stream until thickened. Add nuts; blend 1
or 2 seconds, just to mince. Turn
into a bowl, cover, and chill.

Serve vegetables in a large
basket or crystal bowl. Let
guests make their own selection.
If possible provide each guest
with the aioli dipping sauce in
individual bowls. Makes about 8
appetizer servings.

VARIATION For a dramatic presentation for a large buffet party,
arrange vegetables spilling from
a basket onto the table. Also include wedges of cheese, such as
Gruyère, Fontina, and havarti,
and bunches of red and green
seedless grapes, melon cres-
cents, and pineapple spears.

*Toast pine nuts on a baking
sheet in a 325° F. oven 5 to 7
minutes, or until lightly
browned.

ANTIPASTO

1 cup *each* chili sauce and
  catsup
½ cup *each* water, white wine
  vinegar, and fresh lemon juice
⅓ cup olive oil
2 cloves garlic, minced
1 tablespoon sugar
1 tablespoon *each* Worcestershire sauce and Dijon-style
  mustard
Salt and freshly ground black
  pepper to taste
6 small artichokes
1 dozen small whole boiling onions, peeled
1 fennel bulb, trimmed and cut
  into chunks
1 dozen baby carrots, peeled, or
  4 to 6 small carrots, halved
  and quartered
1 small cauliflower, cut into
  flowerets
½ pound small domestic
  mushrooms
2 cans (7 ounces each) white albacore tuna, drained
1 can (2 ounces) rolled anchovies with capers, drained
Chopped fresh parsley for
  garnish

In a large saucepan combine
chili sauce, catsup, water, vinegar, lemon juice, oil, garlic,
sugar, Worcestershire, and mustard. Bring to a boil and simmer
5 minutes; season with salt and
pepper.
  Peel the outer leaves of the artichokes down to the hearts;
halve and scoop out chokes. Add
to the sauce along with onions
and simmer 10 minutes. Add
fennel, carrots, cauliflower, and
mushrooms; simmer 8 to 10
minutes longer, or until crisp-
tender. Spoon onto a platter,
keeping each kind of vegetable
together; cover and chill. When
ready to serve flake tuna and
add. Garnish with anchovies
and sprinkle with parsley. Makes
12 appetizer servings.

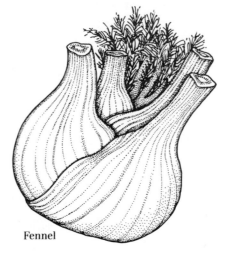

Fennel

BAKED SHIITAKES WITH CHEESE

4 large shiitake mushrooms, stems removed and reserved
2 tablespoons unsalted butter
¼ cup dry white wine
3 tablespoons minced fresh parsley
1 clove garlic, minced
¼ teaspoon dried leaf basil or tarragon, crushed
⅓ cup shredded Fontina or Jarlsberg cheese

Butter a 9-inch pie pan or 4 individual 6-inch ramekins. Slice mushrooms and stems ⅓ inch thick. Arrange in pan or ramekins. In a small saucepan melt butter with wine, parsley, garlic, and basil or tarragon. Pour over mushrooms. Bake in a 400° F. oven 5 minutes. Sprinkle with cheese and bake 2 to 3 minutes longer, or until cheese melts. Makes 4 appetizer servings.

SHIITAKE AND SAUSAGE FRITTATA

2 mild Italian sausages
1 bunch green onions, chopped
2 tablespoons butter
¼ pound shiitake mushrooms (about 1 cup), sliced
2 large bunches spinach, washed, trimmed, dried, and finely chopped
6 eggs, lightly beaten
½ cup sausage broth
Salt and freshly ground black pepper to taste
1 cup shredded Gruyère cheese
½ cup freshly grated Parmesan cheese
¼ cup chopped fresh parsley
1 tablespoon chopped fresh basil
3 cloves garlic, minced
¼ cup sunflower seeds

In a small saucepan poach sausages in water to cover 15 minutes. Drain, reserving ½ cup of the liquid, and let sausages cool slightly. In a large frying pan sauté onions in butter over medium-high heat 1 minute, stirring. Add mushrooms and sauté until glazed, about 2 minutes. Add spinach and cook, stirring, 30 seconds, or just until wilted. Turn into a large bowl. In another medium bowl combine eggs, reserved sausage broth, salt, and pepper. Pour over vegetables; mix in cheeses, parsley, basil, and garlic. Dice sausages and mix in. Turn into a buttered 9- by 13-inch baking pan. Sprinkle with seeds. Bake in a 350° F. oven 25 to 30 minutes, or until set. Serve hot or cold. Makes 6 first-course servings or 2 dozen appetizer squares.

Shiitake

PORCINI AND PROSCIUTTO FRITTATA

¼ pound porcini or shiitake
　mushrooms, sliced
1 shallot, chopped
3 tablespoons butter
6 eggs, lightly beaten
¼ cup freshly grated Parmesan
　cheese
2 teaspoons chopped fresh tarra-
　gon, or ½ teaspoon dried tar-
　ragon, crushed
Salt and freshly ground black
　pepper to taste
3 slices prosciutto, cut in strips

In a medium saucepan sauté
mushrooms and shallot in 2 tablespoons butter until glazed,
about 2 minutes. Remove from
pan and let cool slightly. In a
large bowl combine eggs,
cheese, tarragon, salt, pepper,
prosciutto, and mushrooms. In
an ovenproof skillet heat remaining butter; add egg mixture, reduce heat, and cook until
set, lifting with a spatula to let
egg mixture slip underneath and
cook evenly. Brown lightly under
a broiler. Cut in wedges. Makes 4
servings.

MUSHROOM PARTY PATE

2 leeks (white part only), finely
　chopped
⅓ cup chopped celery
4 tablespoons butter
1 pound mushrooms (combina-
　tion of domestic mushrooms,
　shiitakes, or a few cèpes),
　chopped
2 eggs, lightly beaten
3 ounces natural cream cheese,
　softened
½ teaspoon salt
½ teaspoon dried basil, crushed
¼ teaspoon dried rosemary,
　crushed
¼ teaspoon dried oregano,
　crushed
¼ teaspoon freshly ground black
　pepper
¾ cup fine dry bread crumbs
Watercress or fresh parsley for
　garnish

In a large frying pan sauté leeks
and celery in butter 1 to 2 minutes. Add mushrooms and sauté
until glazed; remove from heat.
In a large bowl combine eggs,
cream cheese, salt, basil, rosemary, oregano, and pepper. Add
mushroom mixture and bread
crumbs and mix well. Turn into
a buttered 9- by 5-inch loaf pan.
Put a strip of waxed paper on top
and cover with foil. Bake in a
325° F. oven 1 hour, or until set.
Cool, then chill. To serve, turn
out of pan and slice. Garnish
with watercress or parsley.
Makes about 16 appetizer
servings.

HOT SHIITAKE AND BACON CHEESE DIP

4 slices bacon, chopped
1 medium onion, minced
½ pound shiitake mushrooms,
　chopped
1 clove garlic, pressed
2 tablespoons all-purpose flour
¼ teaspoon freshly ground black
　pepper
8 ounces natural cream cheese
2 teaspoons soy sauce
2 teaspoons Worcestershire
　sauce
½ cup sour cream
Sliced raw zucchini, jícama, or
　carrots for dipping

In a large frying pan cook bacon
until crisp; remove and drain on
paper towels. Pour out all but 2
tablespoons drippings. Add
onion and sauté a few minutes.
Add mushrooms and garlic and
sauté until limp. Mix in flour and
pepper. Add cheese, soy sauce,
and Worcestershire; stir until
cheese is melted. Remove from
heat and stir in bacon and sour
cream. Serve warm with raw
vegetables. Makes about 2½
cups.

TOASTED WALNUT AND EGGPLANT SPREAD

1 large eggplant (about 1½
    pounds) or the equivalent in
    smaller eggplants
⅛ pound domestic mushrooms
2 green onions, chopped
1 tablespoon olive oil
2 tablespoons fresh lemon juice
3 cloves garlic, chopped
Salt and freshly ground black
    pepper to taste
½ cup plain yogurt
⅓ cup toasted walnuts*
3 tablespoons chopped fresh
    parsley
Cherry tomatoes or yellow plum
    tomatoes
Romaine leaves

Set the whole eggplant in a baking pan; bake, uncovered, in a
400° F. oven 30 to 40 minutes, or
until soft. Dip into cold water.
Prick with a fork and squeeze
out the juices, then peel; cool.
Puree in a food processor or
blender. Sauté mushrooms and
onions in oil until glazed, about
2 minutes, and add to eggplant.
Puree along with lemon juice
and garlic. Season with salt and
pepper and stir in yogurt, nuts,
and parsley; blend just until the
nuts are finely chopped. Spoon
into a bowl and chill. To serve,
spread on halved cherry tomatoes or inner Romaine leaves.
Makes 6 servings.

*Toast walnuts on a baking sheet
in a 325° F. oven 8 to 10 minutes,
or until lightly browned.

TRUFFLED OMELETS

6 eggs
1 small truffle
2 tablespoons butter
¼ pound (1 cup) shredded Gru-
    yère or Jarlsberg cheese
2 tablespoons snipped fresh
    chives

Place eggs in a refrigerator container, add truffle, cover, and
chill overnight (see Note).
    Make individual omelets: For
each omelet beat 3 eggs in a
bowl until blended. Heat 1 tablespoon butter in an omelet pan
until foam subsides; pour in
eggs and cook, lifting from the
edges to let eggs run underneath, until creamy and just set.
Sprinkle with half the cheese
and the chives. Roll up and turn
out on a plate. Shave a little truffle over the top of each. Makes 2
servings.

NOTE The truffle flavor per-
meates the eggs in the shell during refrigeration.

BAGNA CAUDA WITH VEGETABLES AND SAUSAGES

4 Italian sausages (about 1
    pound)
½ cup unsalted butter
1 cup fruity olive oil
4 cloves garlic, minced
4 anchovy fillets, chopped
1 tablespoon minced fresh
    parsley
4 sprigs fresh basil, chopped
Assorted vegetables: fennel, red
    and green bell peppers, baby
    artichoke hearts, small mush-
    rooms, zucchini or golden
    straightneck squash, jícama

Prick sausages in several places
with a fork, place in a baking
pan, and bake in a 350° F. oven
45 minutes, turning once. Meanwhile, using a small fondue pot
or earthenware pot, heat butter,
olive oil, garlic, anchovies, and
basil, stirring to blend. Cut vegetables into bite-sized pieces and
arrange on a platter. Slice sausages and arrange alongside.
Place butter sauce over a
warmer. Use wooden skewers to
pierce vegetables and sausages;
dip into sauce. Makes 6 to 8 appetizer or first-course servings.

VARIATION For individual ser-
vice, halve small sweet red or
yellow bell peppers, core, remove seeds, and fill with Bagna
Cauda sauce. Serve on individual plates, surrounded by vegetables and sausage.

CHEESE RAMEKINS

½ pound Gruyère or samsoe
    cheese
1 fennel bulb, trimmed and
    sliced
12 cocktail sausages
8 boiled new or Finnish potatoes

Slice cheese and place in 4 individual baking dishes or 6-inch
ramekins. Heat in a 350° F. oven
until cheese is melted and starts
to brown, about 10 minutes.
Serve on dinner plates surrounded with fennel, cooked
sausages, and potatoes. Makes 4
servings as a light supper with a
soup or salad.

LITCHI-BACON CRISPS

12 litchis or longans, seeded and
    halved
24 pecan halves
12 bacon slices, halved
⅓ cup soy sauce
⅓ cup packed brown sugar

Fill the cavity of each litchi or
longan with a pecan half. Wrap
½ slice of bacon around each
and secure with toothpicks. Dip
into soy sauce, then roll in
brown sugar. Place on rack set in
a broiler pan and bake in a 400°
F. oven until bacon is crisp,
about 10 minutes. Makes 24
appetizers.

FRESH COCONUT APPETIZERS

1 coconut
1 lime, cut in wedges
Freshly grated nutmeg

To remove the coconut meat
from the shell, pierce one or
more of the "eyes" with an ice
pick. Drain off the liquid. Place
the drained coconut in a baking
pan and bake in a 350° F. oven 15
to 20 minutes. Remove from the
oven and tap with a hammer until cracked in several places.
Separate meat from shell with a
knife. Cut meat into ½-inch
pieces. Serve on a platter, garnished with lime wedges and a
sprinkling of nutmeg. If desired,
toast the coconut slices in a 350°
F. oven 15 minutes, or until
lightly browned. Makes about 3
dozen appetizers.

PAPAYA AND SMOKED MEATS

1 large papaya, peeled, halved,
    and seeded
12 slices prosciutto or salami

Slice papaya into pieces 2 to 3
inches long. Wrap each piece of
papaya in a paper-thin slice of
prosciutto or in a slice of Italian
dry salami. Skewer with a toothpick. Makes about 12 appetizers.

MANGO AND SMOKED SALMON

1 large mango
12 slices smoked salmon

Peel, seed, and slice mango into
2-inch lengths. Wrap each piece
of mango in a slice of smoked
salmon. Skewer with a toothpick.
Makes about 12 appetizers.

Longan

SOUPS

MUSHROOM-LEEK SOUP IN A PUFF PASTRY CAP

2 leeks (white part only), finely chopped
1 carrot, shredded
1 inner stalk celery, finely diced
2 tablespoons butter
¾ pound oyster mushrooms, chopped
2 tablespoons all-purpose flour
3 cups chicken stock (preferably homemade)
1 clove garlic, minced
Salt and freshly ground black pepper to taste
¼ teaspoon dried tarragon, crushed
¾ cup whipping cream or half-and-half
2 ounces chèvre or blue cheese
1 tablespoon minced fresh parsley
1 package (10 ounces) frozen puff pastry shells or equivalent in puff pastry sheets
Egg wash: 1 egg yolk beaten with 1 tablespoon cold water

In a large saucepan sauté leeks, carrot, and celery in butter until vegetables are barely tender. Add mushrooms and sauté 2 minutes longer. Sprinkle with flour and sauté 2 minutes. Stir in chicken stock, garlic, salt, pepper, and tarragon. Bring to a boil, cover, and simmer 15 minutes; cool slightly. Puree in a food processor or blender with cream until smooth. Refrigerate until soup is cold. Ladle into ovenproof cups or bowls to within ½ inch of the top. Crumble cheese over the center of each serving and sprinkle with parsley.

Roll out puff pastry ⅛ inch thick. Cut into rounds ¾ inch larger than the diameter of the soup bowls. Brush edges of the pastry with the egg wash. Place pastry over soup, coated side down. Carefully press edges of pastry against outside edge of cup or bowl. Chill 1 hour to firm up pastry. Brush pastry with egg wash. Bake in a 425° F. oven 15 minutes, or until puffed and golden brown. Serve immediately. Makes 4 servings.

CREAM OF LEEK SOUP WITH BLUE CHEESE

2 cups chopped leeks (white part only)
1 tablespoon minced shallots
2 tablespoons butter
1 cup peeled, diced, raw potato
3 cups chicken stock (preferably homemade)
Salt and freshly ground black pepper to taste
½ teaspoon freshly grated nutmeg
2 egg yolks, lightly blended
½ cup half-and-half
2 tablespoons dry white wine
2 ounces Stilton or Gorgonzola cheese, crumbled, and 2 tablespoons snipped fresh chives for garnish

In a large soup pot sauté leeks and shallots in butter until soft. Add potato and chicken stock, cover, and simmer until potato is tender, about 15 to 20 minutes. Let cool slightly, then puree in a food processor. Season with salt, pepper, and nutmeg. In a large bowl combine eggs and half-and-half. Blend in the hot soup, return to the soup pot, and heat until hot through and thickened, stirring. Stir in wine. Ladle into bowls and garnish with crumbled cheese and chives. Makes 4 servings.

2/3/06 Good w/o eggs ⁴⁄₂₈¹⁄₂

CATALONIAN PEPPER AND LEEK SOUP

3 ounces smoked ham, diced
2 tablespoons olive oil
2 cups diced leeks (white part only)
2 cups thinly sliced leeks (white part only)
½ cup *each* diced sweet red, gold, and green bell peppers
4 cloves garlic, minced
1 tablespoon all-purpose flour
1 quart beef stock (preferably homemade)
1 quart hot water
¼ cup long-grain white rice
Pinch saffron
¼ teaspoon dried savory
Salt and freshly ground black pepper to taste
2 egg yolks
¼ cup olive oil

In a large soup pot lightly brown ham in olive oil. Add both diced and sliced leeks and cook until limp, stirring. Add peppers and garlic; cook 4 minutes, stirring occasionally. Sprinkle with flour and cook 1 minute longer. Remove from heat and stir in stock, water, rice, saffron, savory, salt, and pepper. Simmer, partially covered, 20 minutes. Beat egg yolks with a whisk in the bottom of a tureen; beat in olive oil in droplets (as in making an emulsion for mayonnaise). Dribble in about 2 cups of the hot soup and gradually stir in the remainder. Serve immediately. Makes 6 servings.

LEEK AND SORREL SOUP AVGOLEMONO

2 leeks (white part only), chopped
1 small bunch sorrel (about ¾ cup leaves), shredded
1 tablespoon butter
3 cups chicken stock (preferably homemade)
2 eggs
1½ tablespoons fresh lemon juice
4 ounces feta cheese, crumbled, ¼ cup coarsely chopped pistachio nuts, and 2 tablespoons chopped fresh chives for garnish

In a large saucepan sauté leeks and sorrel in butter until glazed and sorrel changes its color, about 5 minutes. Add stock, bring to a boil, and simmer 5 minutes. Puree in a food processor or blender. In a small bowl beat eggs and lemon juice until blended; add a little of the hot soup and whisk. Pour egg mixture into pan, add remaining soup, and cook over very low heat, stirring, until thickened, about 5 minutes. Ladle into bowls and garnish with crumbled cheese, nuts, and chives. Makes 4 servings.

LENTIL AND FENNEL SOUP

1 medium onion, chopped
1 fennel bulb or 2 stalks celery, trimmed and chopped
1 carrot, shredded
1 leek (white part only), chopped
2 tablespoons olive oil
1½ cups quick-cooking lentils
1 bay leaf
1 clove garlic, minced
½ teaspoon salt
Freshly ground black pepper to taste
2 quarts water
3 tablespoons tomato paste
¼ cup red wine vinegar
½ teaspoon dried oregano, crushed
Plain yogurt and snipped fresh chives or parsley for garnish

In a soup pot sauté onion, fennel, carrot, and leek in oil until limp. Add lentils, bay leaf, garlic, salt, pepper, and water. Cover and simmer until tender, about 1 hour, or according to package directions. Add tomato paste, vinegar, and oregano and simmer 20 minutes longer. Serve topped with yogurt and chives. Makes 8 servings.

PLUM TOMATO SOUP

1 onion, chopped
2 stalks fennel or celery, chopped
1 carrot, grated
1 tablespoon *each* butter and vegetable oil
2 cloves garlic, minced
1 can (6 ounces) tomato paste
6 whole cloves, tied in cheesecloth
1 quart chicken stock (preferably homemade)
1 dozen plum tomatoes, stemmed
Salt and freshly ground black pepper to taste
2 tablespoons chopped fresh basil or fennel tops
Plain yogurt or sour cream (or a blend of equal parts) and fresh basil or fennel sprigs for garnish

In a large soup pot sauté onion, fennel, and carrot in butter and oil until limp. Add garlic, tomato paste, cloves, chicken stock, tomatoes, and salt and pepper; simmer 15 minutes. Remove cloves. Let cool slightly and puree in a food processor or blender. Add basil and puree slightly. Serve hot, garnished with sour cream and basil springs. Makes 6 servings.

EARL'S CURRIED VEGETABLE SOUP

2 leeks (white part only), chopped
1 large onion, chopped
2 tablespoons butter
4 cloves garlic, minced
4 carrots, peeled and diced
2 stalks celery cut in 1-inch lengths
3 zucchini or golden zucchini, cut in 1-inch chunks
1½ to 2 teaspoons curry powder
½ teaspoon dried thyme, crushed
1 quart chicken stock (preferably homemade)
½ cup plain yogurt and chutney for garnish

In a large soup pot sauté leeks and onion in butter until very soft, about 15 minutes. Add garlic, carrots, celery or fennel, squash, curry powder, thyme, and chicken stock. Bring to a boil, cover, and simmer 30 to 40 minutes, or until very tender. Cool slightly, then puree in a food processor or blender. Serve warm, at room temperature, or cold, garnished with yogurt and chutney. Makes 8 servings.

SOUPE AU PISTOU

1 quart chicken stock (preferably
  homemade)
1 cup shelled fava beans
1 carrot, sliced
⅓ pound green beans, cut in 1-
  inch lengths
1 leek (white part only), sliced
1 medium zucchini, thinly sliced
1 golden zucchini, thinly sliced
8 sugar snap peas, trimmed, and
  cut in 1-inch lengths
¼ cup shelled green peas
6 plum tomatoes, sliced
Pesto-Parmesan Blend (follows)

In a large soup pot heat stock.
Add fava beans and carrot and
simmer 8 minutes. Add beans,
leek, and zucchini; simmer 5
minutes. Add sugar snap peas,
peas, and tomatoes; simmer 1
minute longer. Ladle into soup
bowls. Top with a spoonful of
Pesto-Parmesan Blend. Makes 4
servings.

PESTO-PARMESAN BLEND In a
medium bowl combine ¼ cup
chopped fresh basil, ¼ cup
freshly grated Parmesan or Romano cheese, 1 tablespoon fruity
olive oil, and 1 clove minced
garlic.

SUNCHOKE AND
MUSHROOM SOUP

¾ pound Jerusalem artichokes
  (sunchokes)
2 tablespoons fresh lemon juice
1 leek (white part only), chopped
2 tablespoons butter
¼ pound oyster or shiitake
  mushrooms, thinly sliced
3 cups chicken stock (preferably
  homemade)
1 clove garlic, minced
½ teaspoon dried thyme,
  crushed
Salt and freshly ground black
  pepper to taste
3 tablespoons dry white wine
½ cup half-and-half or plain
  yogurt
Toasted hazelnuts* or snipped
  fresh chives for garnish

Peel and dice Jerusalem artichokes. Place in a bowl of cold
water with lemon juice to prevent discoloration. In a large
saucepan sauté leeks in butter
until limp. Add mushrooms and
sauté 1 minute. Add Jerusalem
artichokes, stock, garlic, thyme,
salt, and pepper. Cover and simmer 15 to 20 minutes, or until
Jerusalem artichokes are tender;
cool slightly. Puree in a food processor or blender. Stir in wine
and half-and-half or yogurt. Return to the saucepan and heat
through. Ladle into bowls and
garnish with nuts or chives. If
desired, serve chilled. Makes 4
servings.

*Toast hazelnuts on a baking
sheet in a 325° F. oven 8 to 10
minutes, or until lightly
browned.

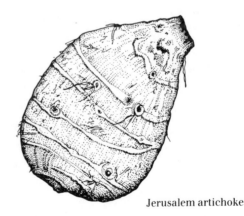

Jerusalem artichoke

FRUITED VEGETABLE SOUP

1 large onion, chopped
1 small bulb fennel or 3 stalks celery, trimmed and chopped
1 carrot, chopped
2 Granny Smith or Golden Delicious apples, peeled, cored, and chopped
1 tablespoon butter
1 quart chicken stock (preferably homemade)
1 dozen yellow or red plum tomatoes, halved
2 cloves garlic, minced
Salt and freshly ground black pepper to taste
6 whole cloves (tied in cheesecloth)
3 tablespoons dry white wine
Plain yogurt or sour cream, snipped fresh chives, and chive blossoms for garnish

In a large soup pot sauté onion, fennel, carrot, and apples in butter until glazed and limp, about 10 minutes. Add stock, tomatoes, garlic, salt, pepper, and cloves; cover and simmer 20 minutes. Let cool slightly; remove cloves. Puree in a food processor or blender; stir in wine. Ladle into bowls and top with yogurt, snipped chives, and a chive blossom. Makes 4 to 6 servings.

CHICKEN-KOHLRABI SOUP WITH PESTO

1½ quarts chicken stock (preferably homemade)
1 onion, quartered
¼ cup celery leaves
1 broiler-fryer chicken (about 3 pounds)
Salt and freshly ground black pepper to taste
3 carrots, peeled and sliced
2 leeks (white part only), chopped
1 stalk celery, chopped
2 medium kohlrabis, peeled and diced
Pesto Sauce (follows)
1 cup shredded Gruyère or Jarlsberg cheese

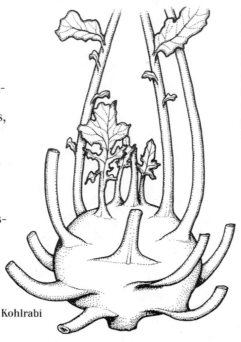

Kohlrabi

In a large soup pot bring stock to a boil; add onion, celery leaves, and whole chicken. Season with salt and pepper, cover, and simmer 1 hour, or until chicken is tender. Remove from pot and let cool slightly. Remove skin and bones and cut meat into large strips and reserve. Skim fat from stock, strain stock, and return to pot.

Bring stock to a boil and add carrots, leeks, celery, and kohlrabis. Cover and simmer 15 minutes, or until vegetables are crisp-tender. Add chicken strips and heat through. Ladle into soup bowls and pass bowls of Pesto Sauce and cheese separately. Makes 6 servings.

PESTO SAUCE In a food processor puree 1½ cups lightly packed, fresh basil leaves, 2 minced garlic cloves, 2 tablespoons parsley sprigs, 3 tablespoons freshly grated Parmesan cheese, ⅛ teaspoon freshly ground black pepper, and ¼ cup olive oil.

MOROCCAN CHARD AND MEATBALL SOUP

Meatballs (follows)
1 bunch red Swiss chard
1 onion, chopped
1 carrot, shredded
1 stalk fennel or celery, chopped
1 tablespoon olive oil
1 teaspoon grated fresh ginger
    root
½ teaspoon *each* ground cumin
    and freshly ground black
    pepper
1½ quarts beef stock (preferably
    homemade)
3 tablespoons tomato paste
6 red or yellow plum tomatoes,
    sliced
Salt to taste
¼ cup chopped fresh cilantro for
    garnish

Prepare Meatballs. Remove ribs from Swiss chard; slice thinly. Chop leaves separately; set aside. In a large soup pot sauté chard ribs, onion, carrot, and fennel in oil until limp. Add ginger root, cumin, pepper, stock and tomato paste; bring to a boil. Cover and simmer 10 minutes. Drop meatballs into the hot broth. Add chopped chard leaves and tomatoes. Simmer 5 minutes longer. Season with salt. Ladle into bowls and sprinkle with cilantro. Makes 6 servings.

MEATBALLS In a medium bowl combine 1 pound lean ground lamb, 3 tablespoons cornstarch, 1 egg, 3 tablespoons minced fresh cilantro, ½ teaspoon ground allspice, and 1 clove garlic, chopped. Shape into ¾-inch balls.

CALDO VERDE

2 large potatoes, peeled and
    sliced
1½ quarts water
Salt and freshly ground black
    pepper to taste
3 tablespoons olive oil
1 bunch kale (about 1 pound),
    cut into strips
½ pound linguica or smoked
    garlic sausage, simmered,
    browned, and thinly sliced
2 tablespoons snipped fresh
    chives and sour cream or plain
    yogurt for garnish

In a large soup pot cook potatoes in boiling water with salt and pepper until tender, about 15 minutes. Mash with a potato masher. Add oil and kale; boil, uncovered, 1 to 2 minutes, or just until crisp-tender. Ladle into soup bowls and top with sliced sausage, chives, and a dollop of sour cream. Makes 6 servings.

HONFLEUR FISH STEW

1 medium onion, chopped
1 leek (white part only), chopped
1 small fennel bulb, trimmed
    and chopped
1 tablespoon butter
1 quart clam or chicken stock
    (preferably homemade)
1 cup dry white wine
2 medium baking potatoes,
    peeled and cut into 1-inch
    pieces
2 carrots, peeled and cut into ½-
    inch pieces
1 bay leaf
½ teaspoon fennel seed
1¼ pounds boneless red snapper,
    halibut or rockfish, cut into
    hefty chunks
Salt and freshly ground black
    pepper to taste
Chopped fennel tops for garnish

In a large soup pot sauté onion, leek, and fennel in butter, stirring, until soft. Add stock and wine and bring to a boil; add potatoes, carrots, bay leaf, and fennel seed. Bring to a boil, cover, and simmer until vegetables are tender, about 15 to 20 minutes. Add fish to soup, cover, and simmer about 5 minutes, or until fish flakes easily with a fork. Season with salt and pepper and ladle into bowls. Sprinkle with fennel tops. Makes 4 servings.

SALADS

HOW TO MAKE
A GREEN SALAD

A creatively assembled green salad is a wonderfully complex and subtle mixture of shades, textures, and tastes. Strive to combine at least three or four varieties of lettuces, both for interesting color and balance of flavors. Mix milder lettuces such as butterheads, romaine, or leaf with stronger-flavored greens such as curly endive, spinach, arugula, dandelion, chicory, or Belgian endive. If possible select greens small enough to be able to use the leaves whole; some chefs believe that cutting or tearing will adversely affect flavor.

Wash greens well, in two soakings of water if necessary; use a salad spinner for drying if you have one. It is important to remove all traces of water that may be clinging to the leaves so that the dressing won't be diluted. Salad greens are delicate; prepare the mixture as close to serving time as possible. Greens can be washed and dried, wrapped gently in paper towels, and stored in a plastic bag in the refrigerator ahead of time, if desired.

When ready to assemble, place greens in a large bowl. Prepare a simple dressing of three parts of a light olive oil to one part good quality wine vinegar, fruit vinegar (as a balance for a very bitter salad), or balsamic vinegar, and salt, and freshly ground pepper to taste. Toss gently and transfer salad to individual serving plates (chefs do this by hand as they believe serving utensils can bruise the greens). Edible flowers such as nasturtium, chive, or arugula blossoms could be used as a garnish, if available.

MARINATED CHARD SALAD

2 bunches red or green Swiss
  chard
¼ cup chopped green onions
Mustard Dressing (follows)
2 hard-cooked eggs, chopped,
  and 1 cup cherry tomatoes,
  stemmed and halved for
  garnish

Wash chard and pat dry. Separate ribs and leaves; slice ribs ¼
inch thick and leaves ½ inch
thick. In a vegetable steamer
cook ribs 3 minutes, add leaves
and cook 7 minutes longer. Remove and cool to room temperature. In a large bowl combine
chard and onions and toss lightly
with Mustard Dressing. Refrigerate 2 hours, or overnight.
Serve garnished with chopped
eggs and halved cherry tomatoes. Makes 6 servings.

MUSTARD DRESSING In a small
bowl or jar with a lid mix together ½ cup safflower oil, 3 tablespoons white wine vinegar, ½
teaspoon salt, ¼ teaspoon
ground cumin, 2 cloves pressed
garlic, 3 tablespoons Dijon-style
mustard, and ¼ teaspoon freshly
ground black pepper. Cover and
refrigerate.

FIDDLEHEAD AND TOASTED WALNUT SALAD

12 fiddlehead ferns
Walnut-Mustard Dressing
  (follows)
2 small heads butterhead lettuce
  (such as Bibb), or red or green
  oak leaf lettuce, leaves separated and torn into bite-sized
  pieces
1 tablespoon *each* finely snipped
  fresh chives and chopped
  parsley
½ cup toasted walnut halves or
  pecans*
4 ounces chèvre, or Campanzola
  or other blue cheese

Wash fiddlehead shoots under
running water to remove brown
covering; drain. In a small
saucepan blanch 2 minutes;
drain and chill. Prepare Walnut-
Mustard Dressing. Place lettuce
in a salad bowl. Add the chives
and parsley. Pour over dressing
and toss lightly. Transfer to individual salad plates and distribute walnuts and fiddleheads over
each. Top with a piece of cheese.
Makes 4 servings.

WALNUT-MUSTARD DRESSING In
a small bowl combine ¼ cup
walnut oil, 1½ tablespoons fresh
lemon juice, 1 tablespoon Dijon-
style mustard, 1 minced shallot,
salt and freshly ground black
pepper to taste.

*Toast nuts on a baking sheet in
a 325° F. oven 8 to 10 minutes, or
until lightly browned.

CELERIAC SALAD DIJON

1 large celeriac (celery root)
1½ teaspoons fresh lemon juice
2 tablespoons Dijon-style
  mustard
6 tablespoons safflower oil
2 tablespoons white wine
  vinegar
Salt and freshly ground black
  pepper to taste
½ teaspoon dried thyme or tarragon, crushed
Butter lettuce, Belgian endive, or
  watercress, separated into
  leaves or sprigs
3 tablespoons *each* chopped
  fresh parsley and capers for
  garnish

Peel celeriac and cut into match-
stick pieces. Cook in boiling,
salted water with lemon juice 2
minutes; drain and cool. Place
mustard in a blender; with motor
running gradually pour in the
oil. Mix in vinegar; add salt, pepper, and thyme. Pour over celeriac and refrigerate, covered, 2 to
3 hours. Serve on a bed of butter
lettuce, endive, or watercress
and sprinkle with parsley and
capers. Makes 4 servings.

VARIATION If desired, garnish
with cooked tiny bay shrimp,
cherry tomatoes, quartered
hard-cooked eggs, and Mediterranean-style olives.

SALAD SAVOY WITH GINGER VINAIGRETTE

1 small head salad savoy (orna-
    mental kale), shredded
2 green onions, chopped
½ cup bean sprouts
1 small sweet red, gold, or pur-
    ple bell pepper, cored, seeded,
    and julienned
Ginger Vinaigrette (follows)
1 dozen yellow plum tomatoes,
    halved
3 tablespoons toasted slivered al-
    monds or toasted sesame
    seeds for garnish*

In a large bowl place the shredded kale, onions, bean sprouts,
and pepper. Pour over Ginger Vinaigrette and mix well. Ring
with plum tomatoes and sprinkle with nuts. Makes 4 servings.

GINGER VINAIGRETTE In a small
bowl combine ¼ cup safflower
oil, 1 tablespoon sesame oil, 1 tablespoon rice wine vinegar, 1 tablespoon lime juice, and 1 teaspoon *each* soy and grated fresh
ginger root. Season with freshly
ground black pepper to taste.

*Toast nuts or seeds on a baking
sheet in a 325° F. oven 8 to 10
minutes for nuts or 5 minutes for
sesame seeds, or until golden
brown.

MARINATED KALE SALAD

1 bunch kale or broccoli rabe
    (about 1 pound), trimmed and
    tough stems discarded
2 green onions, chopped
Cumin-Mustard Vinaigrette
    (follows)
Red leaf lettuce, separated into
    leaves
1 hard-cooked egg, chopped for
    garnish

Cut leaves and stems of greens
crosswise into 1-inch pieces.
Steam 6 to 8 minutes, or until
crisp-tender. Remove to a bowl
and cool to room temperature.
Mix in onions and Cumin-Mustard Vinaigrette. Chill at least 2
hours, or overnight. Serve on leaf
lettuce and garnish with egg.
Makes 4 servings.

CUMIN-MUSTARD VINAIGRETTE
In a small bowl or jar with a lid
mix together ⅓ cup vegetable
oil, 2 tablespoons white wine
vinegar, ¼ teaspoon *each* salt,
black pepper, and cumin, 1 clove
minced garlic, and 1 teaspoon
Dijon-style mustard.

SPINACH AND ENOKI SALAD

2 large bunches spinach,
    washed, trimmed, and dried
4 ounces alfalfa or clover sprouts
1 cup cherry tomatoes, stemmed
    and halved
Curry Dressing (follows)
4 ounces enoki or domestic
    mushrooms, sliced
2 tablespoons toasted chopped
    pecans, walnuts, or sunflower
    seeds for garnish*

Tear spinach into bite-sized
pieces, discarding stems, and
place in a salad bowl. Add the
sprouts and tomatoes and chill
until serving time. To serve, pour
over the Curry Dressing and
scatter the enoki mushrooms
and nuts on top. Makes 6
servings.

CURRY DRESSING In a small
bowl or jar with a lid mix together ½ cup safflower oil, ¼
cup white wine vinegar, 2 tablespoons dry white wine, 2 teaspoons soy sauce, 1 teaspoon dry
mustard, 1 teaspoon curry powder, ½ teaspoon sugar, and ¼
teaspoon freshly ground pepper.

*Toast nuts or seeds on a baking
sheet in a 325° F. oven 8 to 10
minutes, or until lightly
browned.

FLORENTINE SALAD

½ cup olive oil
3 tablespoons red wine vinegar
1 clove garlic, minced
Salt and freshly ground black
    pepper to taste
2 teaspoons chopped fresh basil
    or tarragon, or ½ teaspoon
    dried basil or tarragon,
    crushed
1 cup *each* yellow and red plum
    tomatoes, halved
2 bunches spinach, washed,
    trimmed, and dried
2 heads Belgian endive, sepa-
    rated into leaves
2 hard-cooked eggs, sieved, and
    4 slices crisp-cooked bacon,
    crumbled for garnish

In a small bowl combine the oil,
vinegar, garlic, salt, pepper, and
basil. Add tomatoes and marinate 1 hour. In a serving bowl
place spinach, then tomatoes
and dressing and toss lightly.
Ring with spokes of endive;
sprinkle with eggs and bacon.
Makes 6 to 8 servings.

FENNEL AND BLUE CHEESE SALAD

2 large fennel bulbs, trimmed
    and thinly sliced
1 small cucumber
6 radishes
Vinaigrette (follows)
Curly endive, separated into
    leaves
3 ounces blue cheese, crumbled
1 dozen cherry tomatoes,
    stemmed and halved
1 dozen yellow plum tomatoes,
    halved
1 dozen Mediterranean-style
    olives

Place fennel in a bowl. Peel cucumber and halve lengthwise,
then slice crosswise and add to
bowl. Trim and slice radishes
and add. Pour over dressing and
toss well. Spoon onto curly endive, arranged on a flat platter,
and scatter cheese over it. Ring
with tomatoes and olives. Makes
6 servings.

VINAIGRETTE   In a small bowl or
jar with a lid mix together ⅓ cup
olive oil, 2 tablespoons white
wine vinegar, 1 tablespoon fresh
lemon juice, 2 teaspoons Dijon-
style mustard, 1 chopped green
onion or shallot, 2 tablespoons
chopped parsley, salt and freshly
ground black pepper to taste.

MARINATED SHIITAKES

¾ pound shiitake mushrooms,
    caps and stems thinly sliced or
    stems reserved for another use
2 shallots, finely chopped
1 tablespoon snipped fresh
    chives
⅓ cup olive oil
2 tablespoons white wine
    vinegar
2 tablespoons dry vermouth
1 teaspoon grated lemon peel
Salt and freshly ground black
    pepper to taste
1 bunch radicchio, separated
    into leaves
1 bunch watercress, stems
    removed
2 tablespoons minced fresh
    parsley

Place mushrooms in a large
bowl. In a small bowl mix shallots and chives with oil, vinegar,
vermouth, lemon peel, salt, and
pepper. Pour over mushrooms
and chill 1 hour, stirring several
times. Line four plates with radicchio leaves and watercress
sprigs; spoon the mushrooms
over the greens. Sprinkle with
parsley. Makes 4 servings.

MEXICAN TRAY SALAD

1 large cucumber, scored and
   sliced
3 tablespoons white wine
   vinegar
1 tablespoon olive oil
Salt and freshly ground black
   pepper to taste
Butter lettuce leaves
1 papaya, peeled, seeded, and
   sliced
1 cup peeled, sliced jícama
1 sweet red onion, peeled and
   sliced
1 large ripe avocado, peeled,
   seeded, sliced, and drizzled
   with fresh lemon juice
3 navel oranges, peeled and
   thinly sliced, or 2 sweet red
   bell peppers, cored, seeded,
   and sliced
Spicy Orange Dressing (follows)

In a small bowl mix cucumber
with vinegar, oil, salt, and pepper; let stand 1 hour. Line a large
tray with lettuce; arrange in separate sections the cucumber
(use slotted spoon), papaya, jícama, onion, avocado, and oranges or peppers. Spoon over
Spicy Orange Dressing. Makes 6
servings.

SPICY ORANGE DRESSING In a
small bowl mix together ¼ cup
fresh orange juice, 1 teaspoon
grated lemon peel, ½ teaspoon
crushed dried oregano, and
dash of garlic salt and cayenne
pepper.

ROASTED RED AND GOLD PEPPER SALAD

3 *each* sweet red and gold bell
   peppers, roasted, peeled, and
   seeded (page 39)
¼ cup olive oil
3 tablespoons fresh lemon juice
Salt and freshly ground black
   pepper to taste
½ cup fresh basil leaves
3 ounces chèvre, crumbled

Slice the roasted peppers lengthwise into strips about ¼ inch
wide and place in a large bowl.
Pour over oil, lemon juice, salt,
and pepper; let stand 30 minutes.
Just before serving, reserve a
few basil sprigs for garnish and
chop the remainder. Arrange
peppers on individual plates.
Scatter basil over the peppers
and then top with cheese. Garnish with basil sprigs. Makes 6
servings.

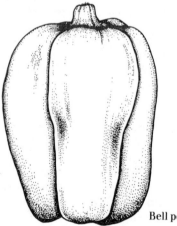

Bell pepper

CUCUMBER, LITCHI, AND GRAPE SALAD

2 medium cucumbers, peeled, seeded, and diced
Salt
1 cup plain yogurt
1 clove garlic, minced
1 tablespoon white vinegar
Salt and freshly ground black pepper to taste
1 green onion, chopped
3 mint leaves, chopped
1 cup seedless red grapes
1 cup seeded litchis or longans
Romaine or grape leaves*
Fresh mint sprigs for garnish

Sprinkle diced cucumbers with salt and let stand 15 minutes for juices to exude; rinse under running water and let drain on paper towels. In a large bowl combine the yogurt, garlic, vinegar, salt, pepper, onion, and chopped mint. Add the cucumbers, grapes, and litchis; chill. Serve on romaine or grape leaves and garnish with mint sprigs. Makes 4 servings.

*Grape leaves are available at specialty food stores and well-stocked supermarkets.

HARVEST SALAD

1 head butter or red or green leaf lettuce, leaves separated and torn into bite-sized pieces
1 Red Bartlett pear, diced
1 sweet red bell pepper, cored, seeded, and diced
1 Granny Smith apple, cored, seeded, and diced
12 small yellow plum tomatoes, halved
2 stalks fennel, chopped
Wine Vinegar Dressing (follows)
¼ cup salted sunflower seeds or chopped toasted hazelnuts*
1 cup alfalfa sprouts
½ cup shredded Gruyère or Jarlsberg cheese

Place lettuce in a bowl. Add diced pear, pepper, apple, tomatoes, and fennel to the greens. Pour the dressing over all and toss lightly. Sprinkle with sunflower seeds, alfalfa sprouts, and cheese. Makes 6 servings.

WINE VINEGAR DRESSING In a small bowl or jar with a lid combine ⅓ cup olive oil, 2 tablespoons red wine vinegar, 2 teaspoons Dijon-style mustard, 1 chopped shallot or green onion, salt, freshly ground black pepper to taste, and 1 teaspoon chopped fresh tarragon or ¼ teaspoon crushed dried tarragon.

*Toast hazelnuts on a baking sheet in a 325° F. oven 8 to 10 minutes, or until lightly browned.

GARDEN GREENS WITH PEAR AND HAZELNUTS

Assorted greens: arugula, mâche, oak leaf lettuce, washed and torn into bite-sized pieces (about 4 cups)
Raspberry Vinaigrette (follows)
1 Red Bartlett pear
3 ounces Bavarian blue cheese (optional)
4 nasturtium blossoms or 12 violets for edible garnish
3 tablespoons toasted chopped hazelnuts*

Place greens in a bowl and pour over Raspberry Vinaigrette; mix lightly. Spoon onto salad plates. Halve, core, and slice pear and arrange on top of each salad. Garnish each with a piece of cheese, if desired, and blossoms. Sprinkle with nuts. Makes 4 servings.

RASPBERRY VINAIGRETTE In a small bowl or jar with a lid mix together ⅓ cup olive oil, 2 tablespoons raspberry vinegar, 2 teaspoons Dijon-style mustard, and salt and freshly ground black pepper to taste.

*Toast nuts in a preheated 325° F. oven 8 to 10 minutes, or until lightly browned.

TABBOULEH IN A FRUIT WREATH

1 cup finely ground cracked
    wheat
1 bunch green onions, chopped
1 cup chopped fresh parsley
½ cup lightly packed chopped
    fresh mint leaves
6 tablespoons olive oil
¼ cup fresh lemon juice
½ teaspoon salt
1 teaspoon ground allspice
¼ teaspoon *each* ground cumin
    and freshly ground black
    pepper
½ cup toasted pecans or
    walnuts*
Grape leaves** or red leaf lettuce
    leaves
Fruit garland: sliced papaya,
    pepino, carambola, kiwifruit,
    strawberries, and seedless
    grapes

Place cracked wheat in a sieve and wash under cold running water. Turn into a bowl and add enough water to cover by one inch. Let stand 1 hour, or until plumped. Drain off any extra liquid. Add onions, parsley, and mint to plumped wheat. Mix together oil, lemon juice, salt, allspice, cumin, and pepper. Pour dressing over wheat mixture and mix lightly. Mix in nuts. Line a large platter with grape leaves or lettuce. Mound salad in the center and ring the outer edge with fruits. Makes 6 servings.

*Toast nuts on a baking sheet in a 325° F. oven 8 to 10 minutes, or until lightly browned.

**Available at specialty food stores and well-stocked supermarkets.

POMEGRANATE WALDORF SALAD

2 cups diced apples or pears
1 cup diced celery
½ cup toasted chopped walnuts,
    or pecans, or sunflower seeds*
2 tablespoons *each* mayonnaise
    and sour cream or yogurt
1 tablespoon fresh lemon juice
1 teaspoon grated lemon peel
¼ cup pomegranate seeds
Butter lettuce or red leaf lettuce,
    leaves separated

In a large bowl combine the apples, celery, and walnuts. In a small bowl stir together mayonnaise, sour cream, lemon juice, and lemon peel and mix in. Scatter over the pomegranate seeds. Spoon onto lettuce leaves. Makes 4 servings.

*Toast nuts on a baking sheet in a 325° F. oven 8 to 10 minutes, or until lightly browned.

Pomegranate

HOLIDAY PERSIMMON SALAD

2 bunches watercress, stems removed
1 large avocado
1 large pink grapefruit
2 persimmons
Balsamic Vinaigrette (follows)

Arrange watercress sprigs on a large platter. Peel and seed avocado and slice lengthwise. Peel grapefruit and cut into segments. Slice persimmons. Alternate wedges of avocado, grapefruit, and persimmon on the watercress. Spoon over vinaigrette. Makes 4 servings.

BALSAMIC VINAIGRETTE In a small bowl stir together ¼ cup safflower oil, 1 teaspoon Dijon-style mustard, 1 teaspoon chopped shallot, and 1 tablespoon balsamic vinegar.

CARAMBOLA FRUIT SALAD

2 large oranges, peeled and thinly sliced
1 cup *each* red and green seedless grapes
1 carambola, mango, or pepino
1 cup watercress leaves
1 large Bermuda onion, thinly sliced
¾ cup feta cheese, broken into chunks
Mint Vinaigrette (follows)

In a bowl combine the oranges and grapes. Slice carambola or peel and slice mango or pepino, and add to the other fruit. Add watercress leaves, onion, and cheese. Pour dressing over fruit; mix lightly. Makes 4 to 6 servings.

MINT VINAIGRETTE In a small bowl combine 3 tablespoons olive oil, 1½ tablespoons fresh lemon juice or raspberry vinegar, 2 tablespoons finely chopped fresh mint, and salt and freshly ground black pepper to taste.

FUSILLI SALAD WITH PEPPERS AND TUNA

½ pound fusilli (pasta twists or spirals), cooked al dente and drained
1 cup yellow or red plum tomatoes, halved
1 *each* sweet red and gold or purple bell peppers, cored, seeded, and julienned
2 cloves garlic, minced
1 small red onion, chopped
¼ cup chopped fresh basil
¼ cup chopped fresh parsley
1 can (7 ounces) white albacore tuna, drained and flaked
Freshly ground black pepper to taste
¼ cup fresh lime juice
⅓ cup olive oil

Place fusilli in a large bowl; add tomatoes, peppers, garlic, onion, basil, parsley, tuna, and pepper. Beat together the lime juice and oil, pour over and mix lightly. Makes 4 servings.

MUSSEL AND VEGETABLE SALAD

1 pound green beans, French-cut or haricots verts, trimmed
1 pound domestic mushrooms, sliced
1 red onion, sliced into rings
½ cup peeled, sliced jícama
⅓ cup olive oil
3 tablespoons red wine vinegar
1 tablespoon Dijon-style mustard
2 teaspoons chopped fresh tarragon, or ½ teaspoon dried tarragon, crushed
Salt and freshly ground black pepper to taste
1 clove garlic, minced
Assorted salad greens
¾ pound cooked mussels, medium shrimp, or scallops
2 hard-cooked egg yolks and 2 tablespoons chopped fresh parsley for garnish

In a medium saucepan cook beans in boiling, salted water to cover 3 to 5 minutes, or until just crisp-tender; drain and rinse under cold running water. Place in a large bowl and add mushrooms, onion rings, and jícama. In a jar with a lid shake together oil, vinegar, mustard, tarragon, salt, pepper, and garlic. Pour over vegetables and mix lightly. Chill 1 hour. Arrange greens on a platter and spoon marinated vegetables on top; ring with your choice of cooked seafood. Sieve egg yolk over the top and sprinkle with parsley. Makes 6 servings.

SQUID AND FENNEL SALAD

2 pounds small squid, cleaned
¼ cup olive oil
1½ tablespoons fresh lemon juice
2 teaspoons chopped fresh fennel tops, or ½ teaspoon dried dill weed, crushed
2 tablespoons minced fresh parsley
Salt and freshly ground black pepper to taste
2 fennel bulbs, trimmed and thinly sliced
2 green onions, chopped
1 small sweet red bell pepper, cored, seeded, and diced
½ cup mayonnaise
2 tablespoons white wine vinegar
2 teaspoons anchovy paste
Leaf lettuce leaves
3 hard-cooked eggs, quartered
3 tomatoes, cut in wedges

Bring a large pot of salted water to a rapid boil; add squid and boil until tender, about 15 to 20 minutes. Drain, cool, and dice. In a medium bowl mix together olive oil, lemon juice, fennel tops, parsley, salt, and pepper. Add squid and marinate 2 hours or longer. Just before serving mix in fennel, onions, and pepper. Combine mayonnaise, vinegar, and anchovy paste; stir in. Arrange lettuce leaves on a platter and spoon squid in the center. Ring with wedges of eggs and tomatoes.

PAPAYA AND SHRIMP SALAD

1 head romaine, leaves separated and torn into bite-sized pieces (about 3 to 4 cups)
1 bunch watercress, stems removed
1 bunch Belgian endive, leaves separated
1 small papaya, peeled, seeded, and sliced
1 avocado, peeled, seeded, and sliced
¾ pound cooked tiny bay shrimp
Chili Dressing (follows)

Place lettuce in a salad bowl; top with watercress leaves. Arrange endive in spokes on top. Alternate papaya and avocado slices in a pinwheel. Mound shrimp in the center. Pour over Chili Dressing and toss at the table.

CHILI DRESSING In a small bowl or jar with a lid mix together ⅓ cup olive oil, 3 tablespoons *each* tarragon-flavored white wine vinegar and chili sauce, salt, and freshly ground black pepper to taste. Add a dash of liquid hot pepper sauce or Angostura bitters. Cover and chill.

VARIATION If desired, substitute mango and kiwifruit or pepino and carambola for papaya and avocado.

CONTEMPORARY COBB SALAD

1 head romaine (pale inner head only), leaves separated and finely shredded
½ head curly endive, leaves separated and finely shredded
½ bunch watercress
2 whole chicken breasts, halved, boned, skinned, cooked, and chilled
2 tomatoes, peeled, seeded, and diced
1 avocado, peeled and diced
1 fennel bulb, trimmed and diced
1 cup alfalfa sprouts or clover sprouts
¾ cup sliced domestic mushrooms
Vinaigrette Dressing (follows)
½ cup crumbled blue cheese and 2 hard-cooked eggs, grated for garnish

In a medium bowl toss together romaine, endive, and watercress leaves. Arrange in nests on 4 large plates. Layer on chicken, tomatoes, avocado, fennel, sprouts, and mushrooms. Just before serving spoon over Vinaigrette Dressing and top with cheese and shredded eggs. Makes 4 servings.

VINAIGRETTE DRESSING In a small bowl combine ¼ cup olive oil, 1 teaspoon Dijon-style mustard, 1 tablespoon balsamic vinegar, 1 chopped shallot, salt, and freshly ground black pepper to taste.

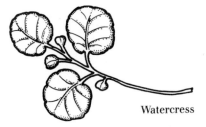

Watercress

CHINESE CHICKEN SALAD

2 whole chicken breasts, halved, boned, skinned, cooked, and torn into strips
Sesame-Soy Dressing (follows)
2 cups shredded Napa cabbage
1 bunch fresh cilantro, stems removed
⅓ cup peeled, slivered jícama
2 green onions, cut in ½-inch lengths and the green ends snipped to resemble fans
3 tablespoons toasted sesame seeds*
⅓ cup toasted slivered blanched almonds*
1 kiwifruit, peeled and sliced
4 litchis or longans, halved and seeded (optional)

Chill chicken. At serving time place chicken strips in a large bowl. Cover with half the dressing; mix well. Add cabbage, cilantro, jícama, onions, sesame seeds, and almonds. Add remaining dressing and mix lightly. Divide evenly among salad plates. Garnish with fruit. Makes 4 servings.

SESAME SOY DRESSING In a small bowl combine ½ teaspoon *each* dry mustard and grated lemon peel, and 2 tablespoons *each* honey, soy sauce, sesame oil, fresh lemon juice, and safflower oil.

NOTE For a pretty presentation use large oriental soup bowls or plates.

*Toast seeds and nuts on a baking sheet in a 325° F. oven 5 minutes for seeds and 8 to 10 minutes for nuts, or until lightly browned.

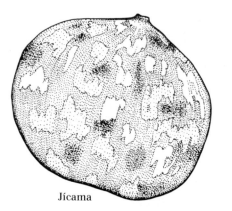
Jícama

TINA'S MANGO CHICKEN SALAD

Mango Vinaigrette (follows)
Assorted greens: butter lettuce,
  red leaf lettuce, mâche
2 whole chicken breasts, halved,
  boned, cooked, and thinly
  sliced
1 *each* avocado, kiwifruit, and
  Red Cuban banana
Seedless grapes (about ¼ pound)
  for garnish

Prepare Mango Vinaigrette and
refrigerate. Arrange assorted
greens on 4 dinner plates. Lay
one sliced breast on each bed of
greens. Peel and slice avocado,
kiwifruit, and banana; arrange
decoratively on each plate. Garnish with a small bunch of
grapes. Pass Mango Vinaigrette
to spoon over. Makes 4 servings.

MANGO VINAIGRETTE In a
blender puree 1 peeled, seeded,
and sliced mango, 2 tablespoons
each walnut oil and raspberry
vinegar, and 1 piece candied ginger in syrup. Pour into a serving
container, cover, and refrigerate.

GRILLED CHICKEN SALAD MARTINIQUE

2 whole chicken breasts, halved
  and boned
¼ cup fresh lemon juice
¼ cup Dijon-style mustard
2 tablespoons minced fresh
  parsley
1 teaspoon chopped fresh
  tarragon
1 green onion or shallot,
  chopped
Salt and freshly ground black
  pepper to taste
1 head red leaf lettuce or
  radicchio, separated into
  leaves
1 bunch mâche or watercress,
  separated into leaves or sprigs
1 *each* avocado, mango, kiwifruit, and feijoa
3 tablespoons fresh lime juice
3 tablespoons olive oil

Marinate chicken breasts in a
mixture of lemon juice, mustard,
parsley, tarragon, onion, salt, and
pepper for 1 hour. Grill over hot
coals or broil, turning to cook
both sides, about 15 minutes, until meat is no longer pink inside.
Slice across the grain, keep each
breast together, and keep warm.
    Meanwhile, line dinner plates
with lettuce and mâche. Peel,
seed (where appropriate), and
slice avocado, mango, kiwifruit,
and feijoa; arrange decoratively
over greens. Combine lime juice
and oil and drizzle over fruit.
Top with hot chicken. Makes 4
servings.

INDIAN CHICKEN IN PAPAYA BOATS

2½ cups diced cooked chicken
½ cups sliced celery
1 cup seedless red or green
  grapes
Chutney Salad Dressing
  (follows)
2 papayas, halved and seeded
3 tablespoons toasted coconut or
  chopped macadamia nuts and
  blossoms for garnish

In a large bowl toss together
diced chicken, celery, grapes,
and Chutney Salad Dressing.
Spoon a mound of salad mixture
into each papaya half and sprinkle with coconut or nuts. Place
on salad plates. Garnish with a
blossom. Makes 4 servings.

CHUTNEY SALAD DRESSING In a
blender container puree ⅓ cup
sour cream, 3 tablespoons mayonnaise, ¼ cup mango chutney
(page 117), 1 teaspoon grated
lemon peel, and 1 tablespoon
fresh lemon or lime juice.

TORTELLINI WITH DRIED TOMATO AND PEPPERONI SAUCE

¼ pound pepperoni, thinly sliced
⅔ cup dried tomatoes (page 116)
1 clove garlic, chopped
1 bunch green onions
2 tablespoons white wine
　vinegar
2 teaspoons Dijon-style mustard
2 teaspoons fresh lemon juice
⅛ teaspoon dried red pepper
　flakes
½ cup olive oil
¾ cup trimmed, diced fennel
　bulb
12 ounces tortellini, cooked al
　dente
2 tablespoons toasted pine nuts*
Cherry tomatoes and fresh basil
　leaves for garnish

In a food processor place the pepperoni, tomatoes, garlic, and white part only of the green onions (chop the green tops and reserve). Add the vinegar, mustard, lemon juice, and red pepper flakes; process until coarsely ground. With motor running add the oil in a thin stream and process until well combined.

In a large bowl place the chopped green onion tops, fennel, and tortellini. Add the sauce and mix until well coated. Sprinkle with pine nuts. Garnish with cherry tomatoes and basil. Serve at room temperature. Makes 4 to 6 servings.

*Toast pine nuts on a baking sheet in a 325° F. oven 5 to 7 minutes, or until lightly browned.

FENNEL AND HOT SAUSAGE SALAD

3 slices sourdough French bread,
　cubed
1 clove garlic, minced
2 tablespoons butter
3 mild Italian sausages
3 thick slices bacon, diced
1 large bunch curly endive or es-
　carole, leaves separated and
　torn into bite-sized pieces
1 fennel bulb, trimmed and
　diced
Shallot Vinaigrette (follows)
1 dozen yellow plum or red
　cherry tomatoes, halved

In a skillet sauté bread cubes and garlic in butter until golden; set aside. In a large skillet simmer sausages in water to cover 20 minutes; drain and slice on the diagonal.

Meanwhile, in a large skillet cook bacon until crisp; drain and reserve (including drippings). Place greens in a salad bowl; add fennel. Pour dressing over greens. Pour on 2 tablespoons reserved hot bacon drippings and mix well. Arrange sausage slices on top and scatter on tomatoes, croutons, and bacon bits. Makes 8 servings.

SHALLOT VINAIGRETTE In a small bowl combine ¼ cup olive oil, 2 tablespoons red wine vinegar, 1 tablespoon Dijon-style mustard, 1 chopped shallot or green onion, salt and freshly ground black pepper to taste.

SPAGHETTI SQUASH WITH ITALIAN MEAT SAUCE

Italian Meat Sauce (follows)
1 spaghetti squash (about 2 to
   2½ pounds)
Salt and freshly ground black
   pepper to taste
½ cup freshly grated Parmesan
   or Romano cheese
1 dozen red and yellow plum
   tomatoes or cherry tomatoes,
   sliced or halved
2 tablespoons chopped fresh parsley or basil

Prepare Italian Meat Sauce. Split squash in half lengthwise. Scoop out seeds. Place, cut-side down, in a large saucepan. Add water to a depth of 2 inches. Cover and simmer 30 to 40 minutes, or until center of squash is crisp-tender. Remove from pan; cool slightly. Using a fork, fluff squash and scoop out spaghetti-like strands. Place strands on a large, warm platter. Season with salt and pepper. Spoon over Italian Meat Sauce and sprinkle with cheese. Ring with tomatoes and sprinkle with parsley or basil. Makes 6 servings.

ITALIAN MEAT SAUCE In a large skillet heat 1 tablespoon olive oil and sauté 1 chopped medium onion. Add 2 cloves minced garlic, 1 pound lean ground beef or ground turkey, and ½ pound ground pork. Sauté until meat loses its pink color. Season with ½ teaspoon salt, ½ teaspoon freshly ground black pepper, and 2 teaspoons *each* fresh or ½ teaspoon *each* crushed dried basil and thyme. Add 1 can (8 ounces) tomato sauce and ⅓ cup dry red wine. Cover and simmer 30 to 40 minutes.

KOREAN BEEF AND VEGETABLES

3 tablespoons soy sauce
1½ teaspoons vinegar
1 clove garlic, minced
1 tablespoon toasted sesame
  seeds, crushed*
1 green onion, minced
1½ tablespoons sesame oil
Freshly ground black pepper to
  taste
1 pound top round steak or flank
  steak, sliced into thin strips
Oil for frying
¼ pound oyster mushrooms,
  torn or sliced into lengthwise
  strips
2 Napa cabbage leaves, cut into
  thin strips
4 green onions, cut into 2-inch
  lengths
2 eggs, beaten slightly
Hot steamed rice for
  accompaniment

In a large bowl combine soy sauce, vinegar, garlic, sesame seeds, onion, oil, and pepper. Add meat, toss to coat, and let sit 1 hour. Using an electric cooker at the table or a wok at stove, heat pan and add enough oil to coat. Sauté vegetables 1 minute; transfer to a hot platter. Clean pan. Reheat with more oil (just to coat); sauté meat 1 minute. Add vegetables and reheat with meat another minute. Stir in eggs and stir briefly. Serve with hot steamed rice. Makes 4 servings.

*Toast sesame seeds on a baking pan in a 325° F. oven 5 minutes, or until lightly toasted.

GREEK STUFFED EGGPLANT

2 medium onions, chopped
1 pound ground lamb
2 tablespoons olive oil
1 carrot, shredded
1 stalk celery or fennel, chopped
⅓ cup chopped fresh parsley
4 to 6 red or yellow plum tomatoes, peeled, seeded, and
  chopped
2 cloves garlic, minced
2 teaspoons chopped fresh basil
½ teaspoon ground allspice
Salt and freshly ground black
  pepper to taste
1 large purple eggplant (about
  1½ pounds) or 2 to 3 smaller
  white eggplants
Salt
2 tablespoons raw long-grain
  white rice

White eggplant

In a large skillet sauté onions and ground meat in oil, stirring until crumbly, until meat is browned. Add carrot, celery, parsley, tomatoes, garlic, basil, allspice, salt, and pepper. Cover and simmer until tender, about 25 minutes. Slice off the stem end of the eggplant to make a lid; scoop out the pulp with a spoon, leaving a shell about 1 inch thick. Sprinkle the inside lightly with salt; set aside. Cube the eggplant pulp and add to the vegetables; simmer 15 minutes longer. Stir in rice. Rinse out the salted eggplant, drain well, and fill with the vegetable mixture. Replace eggplant lid and secure with toothpicks. Place in a deep casserole and fill casserole with ¾ cup water. Cover and bake in a 350° F. oven 1 hour for large eggplant, or 45 minutes for small eggplants. Cut in slices to serve. Makes 6 to 8 servings.

GREEK STUFFED PEPPERS

1 bunch green onions, finely chopped (white part only)
2 tablespoons olive oil
½ cup finely chopped fresh parsley
3 tablespoons short-grain rice
1 large tomato, peeled, seeded, and chopped
1 pound lean ground beef or lamb
Salt and freshly ground black pepper to taste
½ teaspoon dried oregano, crushed
½ teaspoon ground allspice
⅓ cup pine nuts
6 large sweet red, gold, or green bell peppers, tops removed and seeds discarded
2 cups beef stock (preferably homemade)
Lemon Sauce (follows)

In a large skillet sauté onions in oil until limp; add parsley, rice, chopped tomato, meat, salt, pepper, oregano, and allspice. Cover and simmer 20 minutes, stirring occasionally. Mix in pine nuts and, if necessary, cook down until juices evaporate. Spoon into peppers. Arrange stuffed peppers in the skillet, pour in the stock, cover, and simmer 8 to 10 minutes, or until peppers are barely tender. Transfer to a serving platter and keep warm; reserve stock for sauce. Serve surrounded with Lemon Sauce. Makes 6 servings.

LEMON SAUCE Measure reserved stock and add water or cook down to make 2 cups; heat to boiling. Beat 2 eggs until light and blend in 2 tablespoons fresh lemon juice. Pour in the hot stock, stirring constantly; return to pan and heat, stirring, until thickened.

LAMB WITH FENNEL AVGOLEMONO

1½ pounds boneless lamb, cut in
    1½-inch cubes
1 tablespoon butter
1 small onion, finely chopped
Salt and freshly ground black
    pepper to taste
1 teaspoon chopped fennel tops,
    or ¼ teaspoon dried dill weed
1 cup beef stock (preferably
    homemade)
2 fennel bulbs, trimmed and
    quartered
Avgolemono Sauce (follows)

In a large saucepan sauté lamb in butter until meat is browned. Add onion and sauté until golden. Season with salt, pepper, and fennel or dill. Pour in stock and let cook a few minutes, scraping up the drippings. Cover and simmer 1½ hours, or until meat is almost tender.

Add fennel quarters to meat and simmer 15 minutes, or until tender. Prepare Avgolemono Sauce; blend into stew and heat gently, without boiling, until thickened. Makes 4 servings.

AVGOLEMONO SAUCE In a large bowl beat 2 eggs until light and mix in 2 tablespoons fresh lemon juice. Measure the pan juices from the stew and add enough beef stock to make 2 cups. Blend into the egg-lemon mixture.

TURKISH SLASHED EGGPLANT

2 medium onions, chopped
1 tablespoon olive oil
1 pound ground lamb
3 medium tomatoes
3 tablespoons chopped fresh
    parsley
2 cloves garlic, minced
½ teaspoon allspice
½ teaspoon dried oregano,
    crushed
1 tablespoon chopped fresh basil
Salt and freshly ground black
    pepper to taste
8 Japanese eggplants
¼ cup grated Romano or dry
    Jack cheese
½ cup tomato sauce
Basil sprigs for garnish

In a large skillet sauté onions in oil until golden. Add lamb and cook until browned. Peel, seed, and chop 2 tomatoes and add along with parsley, garlic, allspice, oregano, basil, salt, and pepper. Cover and simmer 10 minutes. Slit eggplants lengthwise to within 1 inch of both ends. Place in a baking pan. Cover with foil and bake in a 400° F. oven 30 minutes. Remove from oven and fill each slash with stuffing. Slice remaining tomato and garnish tops of eggplants. Sprinkle with cheese. Pour tomato sauce around eggplants. Cover with foil and bake in a 375° F. oven 30 minutes. Uncover and broil 1 minute. Serve garnished with basil. Makes 4 servings.

MOROCCAN LAMB AND QUINCE TAJINE

1 large onion, chopped
1½ teaspoons chopped fresh gin-
    ger root
⅛ teaspoon ground turmeric
1 cinnamon stick
Salt and freshly ground black
    pepper to taste
1 tablespoon butter
2 cloves garlic, minced
2 pounds lean lamb stew, cut in
    1½-inch cubes
1 or 2 quinces, cored and sliced
1 tablespoon honey
1½ tablespoons fresh lime or
    lemon juice
2 tablespoons chopped pista-
    chios or toasted almonds,* 1
    tablespoon chopped fresh ci-
    lantro, and lime or lemon
    wedges for garnish

In a large ovenproof skillet sauté onion, ginger, turmeric, cinnamon, salt, and pepper in butter until glazed, about 5 minutes. Add garlic and lamb and sauté a few minutes. Cover and bake in a 325° F. oven 1¼ hours. Arrange quince slices on top and bake 30 minutes longer, or until meat is tender. Add honey and lime juice to pan and heat on top of stove, blending in. Sprinkle with nuts and cilantro, and garnish with lime wedges. Makes 6 servings.

*Toast nuts on a baking sheet in a 325° F. oven 8 to 10 minutes, or until lightly browned.

GRILLED ARMENIAN LAMB

1 cup pomegranate juice (freshly squeezed, page 65, or bottled)
1 medium onion, finely chopped
Salt and freshly ground black pepper to taste
4 whole cloves
2 cloves garlic, minced
6 double-rib lamb chops, or 1 small leg of lamb, butterflied (about 3 pounds meat)
Lemon wedges and fresh rosemary sprigs for garnish

In a large bowl combine the pomegranate juice, onion, salt, pepper, cloves, and garlic. Add meat and coat with marinade. Cover and refrigerate 1 day, turning occasionally. Barbecue over medium-hot coals 20 to 30 minutes, until meat is browned but still slightly pink inside. Serve with lemon wedges and rosemary sprigs. Makes 6 servings.

CHAYOTES STUFFED WITH LAMB

4 medium chayotes, halved and seeded
1 small onion, chopped, or 4 green onions, chopped
1 tablespoon safflower oil
2 cloves garlic, minced
1 pound ground lamb or ground turkey
½ teaspoon ground cumin
½ teaspoon ground allspice
Salt and freshly ground black pepper to taste
⅓ cup tomato sauce
3 tablespoons pine nuts or pistachios
2 tablespoons butter
1½ cups shredded Monterey Jack cheese

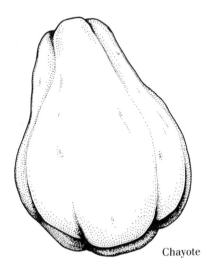

Chayote

Steam chayote halves in a small amount of salted water until just tender, about 10 minutes; drain. Carefully scoop out pulp, leaving a thin, firm shell. Chop the pulp finely, let stand in a bowl for a few minutes, then turn into a colander to drain off any excess liquid.

In a large skillet sauté onion in oil until soft. Add garlic, crumble in meat, and continue to cook until meat is well browned. Add cumin, allspice, salt, pepper, tomato sauce, nuts, and chayote pulp. Continue to cook for 10 to 15 minutes, letting juices evaporate. Lightly fill the chayote shells with the mixture. Dot with butter and sprinkle with cheese. Bake in a 350° F. oven 15 minutes. Makes 4 servings.

ARMENIAN PITA SANDWICHES

1 bunch green onions, chopped
1½ cups cherry tomatoes, stemmed and halved
1 small avocado, peeled, seeded, and diced
4 shiitake mushrooms, sliced or chopped
1 cup alfalfa sprouts
Lemon Dressing (follows)
3 ounces feta or blue cheese, crumbled
4 pita (pocket) breads, halved
½ cup plain yogurt

In a large bowl combine the onions, tomatoes, avocado, mushrooms, and sprouts. Add Lemon Dressing and mix to coat. Mix in cheese. Spoon into split pita breads and add a dollop of yogurt. Makes 4 servings.

LEMON DRESSING In a small bowl mix together 2 tablespoons fresh lemon juice, 1 tablespoon olive oil, 2 tablespoons chopped fresh parsley, salt and freshly ground black pepper to taste, and ½ teaspoon crushed dried oregano.

BARBECUED PORK LOIN WITH PAPAYA AND FEIJOA

1 pound pork loin (about 4 pounds)
½ cup soy sauce
½ cup catsup
¼ cup orange marmalade
2 teaspoons Dijon-style mustard
2 teaspoons chopped fresh ginger root
2 cloves garlic, minced
1 papaya and 2 feijoas, kiwifruit, or carambolas, peeled, seeded, if necessary, and sliced

Marinate the roast in a mixture of soy sauce, catsup, marmalade, mustard, ginger root, and garlic 2 hours or longer. Barbecue over low coals, preferably covered or on a spit, until meat reaches an internal temperature of 165° F. Baste several times with marinade. Carve and serve with fruit and any remaining marinade. Makes 8 servings.

VEAL WITH QUINCE

1½ pounds veal stew
2 tablespoons butter
1 small onion, chopped
Salt and freshly ground black pepper to taste
1 clove garlic, minced
1 cinnamon stick
1 cup chicken stock (preferably homemade)
3 quinces
½ teaspoon grated lemon peel
2 teaspoons brown sugar
2 teaspoons fresh lemon juice

In a large saucepan or Dutch oven sauté meat in 1 tablespoon butter, turning to brown all sides. Add onion and sauté until golden. Add salt, pepper, garlic, cinnamon stick, and stock; cover and simmer 1 hour, or until meat is almost tender.

Meanwhile, halve, core, and slice quinces. In a large frying pan sauté in remaining butter. Sprinkle with lemon peel and brown sugar and cook until fruit is glazed and starts to soften. Arrange on top of meat, sprinkle with lemon juice, and simmer 15 minutes longer, or until meat is tender.

PORK CHOPS WITH PINEAPPLE AND CARAMBOLA

1 tablespoon vegetable oil
4 pork chops
1 small onion, chopped
1 cup diced fresh pineapple
½ cup chicken stock (preferably homemade)
2 tablespoons soy sauce
Salt and freshly ground black pepper to taste
½ teaspoon dried thyme, crushed
1 cup diagonally sliced celery
1 carambola, seeded and sliced

In a large skillet heat oil and brown pork chops on both sides. Add onion and sauté a few minutes. Add pineapple, stock, soy sauce, salt, pepper, and thyme. Cover and simmer until fork-tender, about 40 minutes. If necessary, add additional stock. Add celery and carambola and heat until celery is crisp-tender. Makes 4 servings.

CHICKEN INDIENNE

2 broiler-fryer chickens (about 3 pounds each), quartered
2 tablespoons butter, softened
Salt and freshly ground black pepper to taste
1 cup fresh orange juice
⅓ cup chutney
½ teaspoon ground cinnamon
1 teaspoon curry powder
½ cup chicken stock (preferably homemade)
⅓ cup golden raisins
¼ cup blanched slivered almonds
Fresh fruit garnish (a combination of two or three fruits): sliced pepino, carambola, kiwifruit, seedless grapes, and papaya or mango

Arrange quartered chicken in a greased baking dish. Rub with butter and sprinkle with salt and pepper. Bake in a 425° F. oven 10 minutes. Meanwhile, in a medium saucepan combine the orange juice, chutney, cinnamon, curry powder, chicken stock, and raisins. Simmer, uncovered, until slightly thickened, about 10 minutes. Pour sauce over chicken, reduce temperature to 350° F., and continue baking 35 to 40 minutes longer, or until chicken is tender, basting frequently. Garnish with assorted fruit. Makes 8 servings.

FIVE-SPICE ROAST CHICKEN WITH MANGO

1 broiler-fryer chicken (about 3 pounds)
Salt and freshly ground black pepper to taste
1 teaspoon Chinese five spice*
2 tablespoons soy sauce
2 tablespoons dry sherry
1 teaspoon chopped fresh ginger root
1 clove garlic, minced
1 teaspoon sesame oil
1 mango or papaya, peeled, seeded, and sliced

Rub the chicken with salt, pepper, and five spice, and place on a rack in a baking pan. Roast in a 425° F. oven 15 minutes. In a small bowl combine the soy sauce, sherry, ginger root, garlic, and sesame oil; brush some of the baste over the bird. Reduce heat to 375° F. and roast 1 hour longer, or until drumstick moves easily, basting with remaining sauce. During the last few minutes of roasting, place fruit slices in pan juices and heat until hot through. Transfer bird to a platter, carve, and serve with fruit alongside. Makes 4 servings.

*Available at oriental markets.

TURKEY BURGERS WITH DRIED TOMATOES

1 pound ground turkey
1 egg, or 2 egg whites
2 tablespoons chopped fresh
   parsley
1 green onion or shallot,
   chopped
1 clove garlic, minced
½ teaspoon *each* ground allspice
   and oregano
Salt and freshly ground black
   pepper to taste
2 tablespoons Dijon-style
   mustard
12 dried tomato halves (page
   116)
2 to 3 ounces sliced Jarlsberg or
   Swiss cheese

In a medium bowl combine
ground turkey, egg, parsley, onion, garlic, allspice, oregano,
salt, and pepper. Shape into four
patties. Broil about 3 minutes on
each side, or until browned, yet
still pink inside. Spread with
mustard, distribute tomatoes
over all, and top with cheese. Return to the broiler until cheese
melts. Makes 4 servings.

SNAPPER PACIFIC

3 tablespoons soy sauce
2 tablespoons *each* rice wine or
   dry sherry, fresh lime or
   lemon juice, and peanut or
   safflower oil
1 green onion, chopped
1 teaspoon chopped fresh ginger
   root
1 pound red snapper, shark, sole
   or orange roughy fillets, cut
   into serving pieces
1 papaya or mango, or
   2 kiwifruit or carambolas,
   peeled, seeded, if necessary,
   and thickly sliced

In a shallow dish mix together
the soy sauce, rice wine, lime
juice, oil, onion, and ginger root.
Place fish in marinade and let
stand 30 minutes, turning once.
Drain, reserving marinade, and
place fish on a broiler pan. Broil,
turning once, about 8 minutes or
until golden brown on both sides
and fish flakes when tested with
a fork; transfer to a heated platter. Dip fruit slices in marinade.
Broil until just heated through.
Arrange on fish. Makes 6
servings.

TAMARILLO VARIATION Dip 2 tamarillos in boiling water for 20
seconds; slip off skins. Trim
stem and halve fruit lengthwise
or cut crosswise in thick slices.
Dip in marinade and broil until
heated through.

SNAPPER TAHINI WITH FEIJOA

1 pound snapper or sole fillets
Salt and white pepper
2 tablespoons butter
2 cloves garlic, minced
3 tablespoons tahini*
¼ cup fresh lemon juice
2 tablespoons chopped fresh
   mint
2 feijoas, peeled and sliced
4 small clusters green or red
   seedless grapes and fresh mint
   sprigs for garnish

Place fish on a broiling pan; season with salt and pepper. Melt
butter with garlic and drizzle
over fish. Broil on one side only,
until fish is golden brown and
fish flakes when tested with a
fork. Transfer to a heated platter.
Mix together the tahini, lemon
juice, and chopped mint; spoon
over fish. Garnish with feijoas
and grapes. Tuck in mint sprigs.
Makes 4 servings.

VARIATION Instead of feijoa, substitute mango, kiwifruit, or
pepino.

*Tahini is a ground sesame seed
paste available in Mediterranean
markets or well-stocked
supermarkets.

SAMOAN BUTTER-BROWNED FISH

1 pound orange roughy, mahi-mahi, or sole fillets
3 tablespoons fresh lime or lemon juice
Salt and white pepper to taste
Cornstarch or flour
2 tablespoons butter
¼ cup chopped pistachios or macadamia nuts
1 mango, peeled, seeded, and sliced
1 kiwifruit, peeled and sliced
1 lime or lemon, cut in wedges for garnish

Brush fish with 1 tablespoon of the lime juice, season with salt and pepper, and dust lightly with cornstarch. In a large skillet sauté fish fillets in 1 tablespoon butter, turning to brown both sides, about 8 minutes or until fish flakes when tested with a fork; transfer to a heated platter. In remaining butter sauté nuts until golden brown. Add remaining lime juice, stirring to scrape up drippings, and spoon over fish. Arrange mango and kiwifruit on top and garnish with lime. Makes 4 servings.

MAHI-MAHI WITH PEPINO

1 pound mahi-mahi, swordfish, or other white-fleshed fish fillets
Salt and white pepper to taste
Cornstarch or flour
2 tablespoons butter
1 teaspoon curry powder
2 ripe pepinos or bananas, peeled and sliced
2 tablespoons orange juice concentrate
1 tablespoon chopped pistachio nuts, or 2 tablespoons toasted shredded coconut* and 1 lime or lemon, cut in wedges for garnish

Season fish with salt and pepper and dust lightly with cornstarch. In a large skillet sauté fish in 1 tablespoon butter about 8 minutes, or until fish flakes when tested with a fork; set aside. Melt remaining butter, add curry and pepino or bananas; cook 1 minute. Turn over, add orange juice concentrate, and cook 1 minute longer. Arrange fish on dinner plates, spoon sauce over, and sprinkle with nuts. Garnish with lime wedges. Makes 4 servings.

*Toast nuts or coconut on a baking sheet in a 325° F. oven 8 to 10 minutes, or until lightly browned.

FENNEL AND FISH-STUFFED TOMATOES

¾ pound cold poached snapper, halibut, sole, or turbot
1 fennel bulb, trimmed and diced
¼ cup olive oil
2 tablespoons fresh lemon juice
1 tablespoon white wine vinegar
Salt and freshly ground black pepper to taste
4 leaves fresh mint, chopped
2 green onions, chopped
3 tablespoons chopped fresh parsley
¼ cup dried dill weed
2 tablespoons pine nuts
4 medium tomatoes
Salad greens
1 dozen tiny Mediterranean-style olives for garnish

Flake the fish coarsely into a medium bowl; add diced fennel. Combine the oil, lemon juice, vinegar, salt, pepper, mint, onions, parsley, dill, and pine nuts; add to the fish, mixing lightly. Set aside. Core tomatoes, scoop out the pulp, and reserve pulp for another use. Spoon fish salad into the tomato shells and chill until serving time. Serve on greens and garnish with olives. Makes 4 servings.

VEGETABLES

VEGETABLES A LA GRECQUE

2 cups chicken stock (preferably homemade), or 2 cups water plus 2 teaspoons chicken stock base
½ cup dry vermouth or dry white wine
1 tablespoon fresh lemon juice
2 tablespoons olive oil
3 shallots or green onions, finely chopped
¼ teaspoon dried thyme, crushed
6 peppercorns
2 strips lemon peel, slivered
Vegetables: 1½ pounds mushrooms or assortment of zucchini, golden straightneck, leeks, carrots, fennel, or eggplant*
Chopped fresh parsley for garnish

In a large saucepan combine the stock, vermouth, lemon juice, oil, shallots, thyme, peppercorns, and lemon peel. Cover and simmer 10 minutes. Add prepared vegetables and simmer as directed. Remove vegetables with a slotted spoon and arrange on a serving dish. Rapidly boil down juices until reduced to about ½ cup. Spoon over the vegetables and serve hot or cover and chill. Sprinkle with parsley just before serving. Makes about 6 servings.

*For *mushrooms*, trim and wash. Leave whole if small or quarter or halve if large. Add to the stock and simmer 3 to 4 minutes.

For *zucchini or yellow straightneck*, trim ends. Slice on the diagonal, add to stock, and simmer 3 to 5 minutes, or until crisp-tender.

For *leeks*, trim ends, cut lengthwise, and wash thoroughly. Add to the stock and simmer 8 minutes, or until tender.

For *carrots*, peel and slice on the diagonal about ¼ inch thick. Add to stock, simmer about 10 minutes, or until crisp-tender.

For *fennel*, separate bulb, trim, and cut into triangular pieces. Add to the stock and simmer 8 minutes, or until crisp-tender.

For *eggplant*, cut in lengthwise wedges. Add to stock and simmer 10 minutes.

CURRIED JICAMA AND CARROT SOUFFLE

½ cup grated carrots
½ cup grated jícama or golden
  zucchini, pressed of moisture
2 tablespoons butter
¼ teaspoon salt
¼ teaspoon ground cumin
2 tablespoons all-purpose flour
⅔ cup milk
3 eggs, separated
¼ cup shredded Swiss cheese
Lemon or lime wedges for
  garnish

In a large skillet sauté carrots and jícama in butter until glazed, about 5 minutes. Add salt, cumin, and flour; cook 2 minutes. Add milk and cook until thickened, about 5 minutes. Remove from heat and mix in egg yolks. In a medium bowl beat egg whites until soft peaks form and fold into vegetable mixture with cheese. Turn into a buttered 1-quart soufflé dish. Bake in a 375° F. oven 20 minutes, or until puffed and golden brown. Serve immediately with citrus wedges. Makes 2 to 3 servings.

ARTICHOKE HEARTS WITH LEEKS AND GARLIC

8 medium artichokes
Juice of 1 lemon
2 tablespoons butter
2 tablespoons olive oil
8 leeks (white part only), sliced
1 head garlic, peeled
Salt and freshly ground black
  pepper to taste
½ teaspoon dried thyme,
  crushed
2 tablespoons white wine
  vinegar
Minced fresh parsley for garnish

Peel off most of the outer leaves of the artichokes and discard; cut artichokes in quarters, scrape out the chokes, and remove tough tops. Sprinkle with lemon juice. In a large, covered saucepan simmer artichokes in 1 inch water, butter, oil, leeks, garlic, salt, pepper, and thyme, 20 minutes. Add vinegar, cover, and cook 5 minutes longer. Serve sprinkled with parsley. Makes 8 servings.

CHAYOTE WITH CHEESE AND CHILIES

3 chayotes, peeled and sliced or
  diced (cutting through flat,
  edible inner seed)
1 small onion, chopped
2 garlic cloves, minced
2 medium tomatoes, peeled,
  seeded, and chopped
2 green chili peppers, seeded
  and diced*
¼ teaspoon ground coriander
¼ teaspoon salt
1 tablespoon butter
¼ pound Monterey Jack cheese,
  cut in strips
Fresh cilantro sprigs for garnish

In a medium saucepan combine chayotes, onion, garlic, tomatoes, chilies, coriander, and salt. Cook over low heat, covered, until tender, about 15 minutes. Add butter and stir to coat. Place vegetables in a buttered, 1½-quart baking dish. Top with cheese and broil until cheese melts. Garnish with cilantro sprigs. Makes 6 servings.

*Use caution when handling chilies; keep hands away from eyes and wear gloves.

OPEN SESAME BROCCOLI RABE

1 pound broccoli rabe or Napa cabbage, trimmed and tough stems discarded
Salt and freshly ground black pepper to taste
1 tablespoon sesame oil
2 tablespoons toasted sesame seeds*

Cut broccoli rabe in 1-inch strips. Steam until leaves are crisp-tender, about 6 to 8 minutes. Place in a bowl, season with salt and pepper, drizzle with sesame oil, and toss lightly to blend. Serve sprinkled with sesame seeds. Makes 4 servings.

*Toast seeds on a baking sheet in a 325° F. oven 5 minutes, or until lightly browned.

MUSTARD GREENS SAUTE

1 pound mustard greens, trimmed and tough stems discarded
2 tablespoons olive oil
1 clove garlic, minced
½ teaspoon dried oregano, crushed
1 lemon, cut in wedges

Cut stems and leaves of greens crosswise into 1-inch strips. In a skillet or wok sauté in oil with garlic over medium heat until crisp-tender, about 2 to 4 minutes. Serve with lemon wedges.

LONG BEANS AND WATER CHESTNUTS

1 pound long beans, trimmed and cut in 1-inch lengths
3 green onions, chopped
1 fresh jalapeño pepper, seeded and chopped*
1 clove garlic, minced
⅛-inch slice fresh ginger root, chopped
2 tablespoons vegetable oil
6 water chestnuts, peeled and sliced

In a saucepan cook beans in boiling, salted water until crisp-tender, about 5 minutes; drain well. In a skillet or wok sauté onions, pepper, garlic, and ginger root in oil over medium heat. Add beans and water chestnuts and toss to heat through. Makes 4 servings.

VARIATION While hot, toss beans and water chestnuts with 2 tablespoons *each* rice vinegar and vegetable oil; chill. Serve cold.

*Use caution when handling chilies; keep hands away from eyes and wear gloves.

FENNEL WITH PARMESAN COATING

2 fennel bulbs, trimmed
1 tablespoon each olive oil and butter
¼ teaspoon freshly grated nutmeg
¼ teaspoon freshly grated black pepper
½ cup freshly grated Parmesan or Romano cheese

In a medium saucepan blanch or steam fennel until tender, about 10 to 15 minutes. Cool slightly, then quarter and arrange in a buttered baking dish. Drizzle with olive oil and dot with butter. Season with nutmeg and pepper. Sprinkle with cheese. Broil until cheese melts and browns slightly. Makes 4 servings.

SHREDDED KOHLRABI WITH CHIVES

3 to 4 kohlrabis, peeled and shredded
2 tablespoons butter
⅓ cup chicken stock (preferably homemade)
Salt and freshly ground black pepper to taste
1 tablespoon snipped fresh chives

In a large skillet place the kohlrabis, butter, stock, salt, and pepper. Cover and simmer 3 to 4 minutes, or until crisp-tender. Serve sprinkled with chives. Makes 4 servings.

WHIPPED POTATOES AND KOHLRABI

2 large white potatoes, peeled
  and cut into chunks
2 to 3 kohlrabis, trimmed and
  quartered
2 tablespoons butter
2 tablespoons whipping cream
Salt and freshly ground black
  pepper to taste
¼ teaspoon freshly grated
  nutmeg
1 tablespoon minced fresh
  parsley

Boil potatoes and kohlrabis in
separate pans of boiling, salted
water until tender, about 20 minutes; drain. Skin, and puree the
kohlrabis in a food processor.
Mash the potatoes and whip in
the kohlrabi puree, butter,
cream, salt, pepper, nutmeg, and
parsley. Makes 4 servings.

DAIKON-POTATO PUREE

1 pound daikon radish
1 small potato
¼ cup half-and-half or whipping
  cream
1 tablespoon melted butter
½ teaspoon dried chervil or
  basil, crushed
Freshly grated nutmeg

Peel daikon and potato and cut
into 1½-inch chunks. In a
medium saucepan cook in boiling, salted water for 20 minutes,
or until tender; drain. Puree in a
food processor with half-and-
half, butter, and chervil. Serve
dusted with freshly grated nutmeg. Makes 4 servings.

BRAISED FAVA BEANS

1 bunch green onions, finely
  chopped
2 tablespoons olive oil
1½ pounds fava beans
2 tomatoes, peeled, seeded, and
  chopped
1 clove garlic, minced
3 tablespoons finely chopped
  fresh parsley
Salt and freshly ground black
  pepper to taste

In a heavy saucepan sauté
onions in oil until glazed, about
5 minutes. Trim ends of beans
and cut beans in 1½-inch
lengths. Add to onions along
with tomatoes, garlic, parsley,
salt, and pepper. Cover and simmer 15 to 20 minutes, or until
tender. Makes 6 servings.

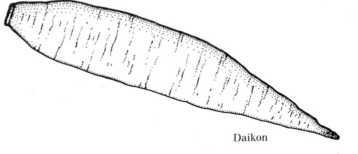

Daikon

BAKED MUSHROOMS WITH HERBS

1 pound shiitake, oyster, or domestic mushrooms (or a combination), sliced
⅓ cup butter, softened
2 tablespoons minced fresh parsley
1 shallot, chopped
1 tablespoon Dijon-style mustard
Salt and freshly ground black pepper to taste
2 teaspoons fresh tarragon, chopped, or ½ teaspoon dried tarragon, crushed
1½ tablespoons all-purpose flour
1 cup whipping cream

In a buttered 1½-quart casserole place a layer of mushrooms. Mix together the butter, parsley, shallot, mustard, salt, pepper, tarragon, and flour and dot the mushrooms with half the butter mixture. Top with remaining mushrooms and butter mixture. Pour cream over all. Bake uncovered in a 350° F. oven 50 minutes, or until cooked through. Serve as an accompaniment to grilled steak or chicken. Makes 4 servings.

BROILED EGGPLANT SESAME

4 small oriental eggplants, halved lengthwise
Salt and freshly ground black pepper to taste
2 tablespoons sesame oil

Season eggplants with salt and pepper and brush lightly with sesame oil. Broil or barbecue until soft and brown, about 5 to 10 minutes. Makes 4 servings.

SHIITAKE PILAF

½ cup thin vermicelli noodles, broken into small lengths
2 tablespoons butter
1 cup long-grain rice
½ cup finely chopped onion
Salt and freshly ground black pepper to taste
2½ cups boiling chicken or beef stock (preferably homemade)
½ cup shiitake mushrooms, chopped coarsely

In a large saucepan brown noodles in butter, stirring constantly. Add rice and stir to coat well with butter. Add onion and cook 2 minutes. Add salt, pepper, and stock. Cover and simmer until rice is fluffy and moisture is absorbed, about 20 minutes. Add shiitakes and fluff. Let stand a few minutes. Makes 4 servings.

SAUTEED SUNCHOKES AND GRAPES

¾ pound Jerusalem artichokes (sunchokes) whole, unpeeled, and scrubbed
1 tablespoon butter
2 tablespoons whipping cream
¼ teaspoon freshly ground black pepper
¼ teaspoon freshly grated nutmeg
1 cup seedless red or green grapes, whole or halved

In a medium saucepan bring 1 inch salted water to a boil, add Jerusalem artichokes, and cook over medium heat until tender, about 15 minutes. Drain, cool slightly, peel, and slice thinly. Melt butter in a large skillet, add Jerusalem artichokes, and sauté to coat lightly. Add cream, pepper, nutmeg, and grapes. Boil, shaking pan, until juices are reduced to a glaze and grapes are heated through, about 2 minutes. Makes 4 servings.

SUGAR-SNAP STIR FRY

1 pound sugar snap peas,
  trimmed and cut in 1-inch
  lengths
2 tablespoons vegetable oil
6 water chestnuts, peeled and
  sliced
1 clove garlic, minced
½ teaspoon grated fresh ginger
  root
½ teaspoon soy sauce
8 sprigs fresh cilantro

In a wok or large skillet stir-fry
peas in oil over medium-high
heat 2 minutes. Add water chestnuts, garlic, ginger root, and soy
sauce; cook 1 to 2 minutes
longer, or until peas are crisp-
tender. Garnish with cilantro
sprigs. Makes 4 servings.

GREEN BEANS WITH JICAMA

1½ pounds green beans,
  trimmed and French-cut or
  haricots verts, trimmed
1 tablespoon butter
½ cup peeled, diced jícama
2 green onions, chopped
½ teaspoon dried tarragon,
  crushed
Salt and freshly ground black
  pepper to taste

Cook beans in a large pot of boiling, salted water until crisp-tender, about 3 to 5 minutes; drain.
Add butter to pan along with jícama, onions, tarragon, salt, and
pepper. Heat, stirring, until vegetables are heated through and
coated with butter. Makes 4
servings.

CARDOONS MILANESE

1½ pounds cardoons
3 tablespoons melted butter
¼ cup freshly grated Parmesan
  or Fontina cheese
Salt and freshly ground black
  pepper to taste
3 tablespoons chopped fresh
  parsley for garnish

Trim away the leafy parts from
the fleshy ribs of the vegetable.
Cut ribs into 2-inch lengths and
drop into a big kettle of boiling,
salted water. Return to a boil and
cook until just barely tender,
about 8 minutes. Arrange cardoons in an ovenproof baking
dish, drizzle with butter, and
sprinkle with cheese, salt, and
pepper. Broil until cheese melts.
Sprinkle with parsley. Serve as
an accompaniment to pasta or
veal. Makes 4 servings.

BOILED CASSAVA WITH ROASTED GARLIC

1 pound cassava
4 heads garlic
2 to 3 tablespoons olive oil
Salt and freshly ground black
  pepper to taste

Peel cassava and cut into 2-inch
lengths. Cook in boiling, salted
water for 1 to 1½ hours, or until
tender; drain.
  Meanwhile, arrange garlic in
a baking dish; drizzle with olive
oil. Bake in a 350° F. oven 1 hour,
or until cloves are soft. Season
cassava with salt and pepper. Offer a head of garlic alongside
each serving; squeeze the garlic
onto the cassava, clove by clove.
Makes 4 servings.

CONDIMENTS & RELISHES

DRIED PLUM TOMATOES

4 pounds red or yellow plum
   tomatoes, washed and
   stemmed
2 teaspoons salt
Olive oil
Fresh rosemary sprigs

Cut tomatoes in half, leaving the
two sides attached. Overlap two
wire racks on large 10- by 15-
inch baking sheets and place tomatoes, cut side up, on the racks.
Sprinkle lightly with salt. Place
in a 200° F. oven and let dry until
shriveled yet still flexible, about
8 hours. Place in a jar and cover
with olive oil and a sprig or two
of rosemary. Store in a dark spot
3 to 4 weeks, turning the jar occasionally. Makes about 1 pint.

PICKLED GARLIC

3 to 4 heads garlic
1 teaspoon sea salt
1 tablespoon whole coriander
   seeds, lightly crushed
4 peppercorns
1 dried chili pepper
Pinch dried tarragon or thyme,
   crushed
Cider or wine vinegar

Peel garlic, if desired, or leave
cloves unpeeled. Place cloves in
a glass jar alternately with salt,
coriander, peppercorns, chili
pepper, and tarragon or thyme.
Pour over enough vinegar to
cover. Cover with a lid and store
in a dark place at least 2 weeks
or up to several months. Serve as
an appetizer accompaniment
along with cheese, cold meats,
and nuts, or as a condiment with
an entree of lamb, pork, or poultry. Makes about 1½ cups.

TOMATILLO SALSA

1 pound green tomatillos
4 small yellow hot chilies
3 green onions (white part only),
   chopped
1 clove garlic, minced
Salt and freshly ground black
   pepper to taste

Place tomatillos in a large saucepan, add a little water, and cover
and simmer until soft, about 15
minutes; peel off husks and
quarter. Puree in a blender with
chilies, onions, garlic, salt, and
pepper. Return to the saucepan,
bring to a boil, and simmer 5
minutes. Cool and chill. Serve as
a condiment with tacos or enchiladas. Makes about 2 cups.

TOMATILLO SALSA FOR PORK

½ pound tomatillos
1 medium onion
½ pound tomatoes
2 cloves garlic, peeled and
  minced
1 cup chicken or pork broth
½ teaspoon salt
½ teaspoon dried red pepper
  flakes
1 teaspoon brown sugar
½ cup fresh cilantro, minced

In a medium saucepan parboil tomatillos in salted water 10 minutes. Peel off husks, cut into quarters, and chop coarsely in a food processor by pulsing. Remove to a large bowl. Peel and quarter onion and chop the same way; add to tomatillos. Peel and quarter tomatoes, chop the same way, and add to tomatillos with minced garlic. Place all ingredients except cilantro in a large saucepan and bring to a boil; reduce heat and simmer 20 minutes. Stir in cilantro and simmer 5 minutes longer. Serve as an accompaniment for pork roast or spareribs. Salsa keeps refrigerated 1 week and freezes several months. Makes 3 cups.

VARIATION If desired, add an equal amount of tomato-based barbecue sauce and spread on barbecued spareribs towards the end of their cooking time.

MANGO CHUTNEY THE BENNETT KITCHEN

5 pounds firm mangoes, peeled,
  seeded, and thinly sliced
2 bell peppers, cored, seeded,
  and chopped
2 large onions, chopped
2 apples, cored and chopped
½ firm papaya, peeled, seeded,
  and chopped
1 lime, thinly sliced and
  quartered
4 ounces candied ginger,
  coarsely chopped
1 tablespoon ground cinnamon
2 teaspoons salt
1 teaspoon ground allspice
1 teaspoon ground cloves
1 teaspoon dried red pepper
  flakes
¼ teaspoon cayenne pepper
5 cloves garlic, pressed
1 cup raisins
1 quart white wine vinegar
3 cups packed brown sugar
1½ tablespoons tamarind
  concentrate*

In a large saucepan add all ingredients except tamarind and bring to a boil; reduce heat and simmer 1 hour. Add tamarind to chutney and simmer 30 minutes longer, stirring frequently. Pack into sterilized jars and seal. Process in boiling water bath 10 minutes. Makes 6 pints.

NOTE For a coarse texture similar to Major Grey's chutney, use slightly green mangoes.

*Tamarind concentrate is available in specialty food stores.

CRANBERRY-KUMQUAT CHUTNEY

8 kumquats, trimmed, cut crosswise into ¼-inch slices, and
  seeded
1 package (12 ounces)
  cranberries
1 cup sugar
1 apple, cored and chopped
⅓ cup apple cider vinegar
½ cup raisins
1 teaspoon finely chopped fresh
  ginger root
1 cinnamon stick
¼ teaspoon dried red pepper
  flakes
¼ cup chopped walnuts or pecans (optional)

In a large saucepan combine kumquats, cranberries, sugar, apple, vinegar, raisins, ginger root, cinnamon stick, and pepper. Bring to a boil, stirring. Reduce heat to simmer and cook, uncovered, until thickened, about 20 minutes. Cool and chill. Serve as an accompaniment to roast turkey, pork, or duck. Makes about 4 cups.

CONFETTI RELISH

6 *each* green, gold, red, and purple bell peppers, cored, seeded, and coarsely chopped
1 jalapeño pepper, cored, seeded, and coarsely chopped*
4 onions, chopped
2 cups sugar
4 cups white or cider vinegar
1 tablespoon mustard seed

Put chopped peppers into a large bowl and cover with boiling water; let stand 10 minutes. Drain and repeat three times. Drain and turn into a large saucepan. Add onions, sugar, vinegar, and mustard seed. Boil 30 minutes. Ladle into hot, sterilized jars; seal and process in boiling water bath 15 minutes. Makes 6 pints.

*Use caution when handling chilies; keep hands away from eyes and wear gloves.

PICKLED QUINCE

8 large quinces, peeled, cored, and quartered
Whole cloves
2 small oranges, sliced
6 cups sugar
1 pint white or cider vinegar
1½ cups quince liquid
1 cinnamon stick (3 inches)

In a large pan steam quinces until tender, remove from steamer, set quinces aside, and save liquid. Measure, and if necessary, add enough water to make 1½ cups liquid. Stick a clove into each quince quarter. In a large saucepan place oranges, sugar, vinegar, quince liquid, and cinnamon stick. Bring to a boil and simmer 10 minutes. Add quinces and cook until translucent, about 30 minutes. Pack fruit into jars, cover with syrup, and seal. Process in boiling water bath 10 minutes. Makes about 6 pints.

GINGERED FRUIT

2 shallots, finely chopped
1 teaspoon finely chopped fresh ginger root
1 tablespoon butter
1 cup peeled, seeded, if necessary, and sliced or quartered fruit: mango, papaya, pepino, kiwifruit, tamarillo, feijoa, or guava
1 tablespoon fresh lime juice
2 teaspoons brown sugar

In a large skillet sauté shallots and ginger root in butter until glazed, about 1 minute. Add fruit and cook until heated through, about 2 to 3 minutes. Add lime juice and sugar and mix gently. Serve hot as an accompaniment to barbecued or roast chicken, turkey, duck, pork, ham, or lamb. Makes 4 servings.

Quince

SUNBURST TART

Press-in Pastry (page 120)
3 ounces natural cream cheese,
  softened
1 tablespoon cognac or brandy
2 tablespoons confectioners'
  sugar
2 tablespoons sour cream
Assorted tropical fruit: carambola, kiwifruit, and mangoes
  or papayas, peeled, seeded if
  necessary, and sliced to make
  about 3 cups
¼ cup apricot jam, pureed

Prepare Press-in Pastry. In a medium bowl beat cream cheese
until creamy, then beat in cognac, sugar, and sour cream.
Spread in baked pastry shell. Arrange fruit in concentric circles
on top. Drizzle with apricot puree. Refrigerate until serving
time. Makes 8 servings.

CARAMELIZED PEAR TART

5 ounces puff pastry*
6 large Red Bartlett pears, cored,
  or tart cooking apples, peeled
  and cored
⅔ cup sugar
⅓ cup water
1 piece (2 inches) vanilla bean,
  split
Whipped cream or ice cream for
  accompaniment

Roll out pastry on a lightly
floured board to a 12-inch circle.
Place in a 10-inch springform
pan, letting the edge roll slightly
up the sides. Prick with a fork.
Freeze 5 minutes to chill thoroughly. Bake in a 450° F. oven 8
to 10 minutes, or until golden
brown. (The shell will shrink
slightly, completely fitting the
bottom of the pan.)

Cut pears or apples into
eighths. In a large skillet bring
⅓ cup of the sugar and the water
to a boil. Add the fruit and vanilla bean; cover and simmer 10
minutes. Remove cover and cook
until fruit is tender and slightly
caramelized and the liquid is
evaporated, about 5 to 10 minutes. Remove vanilla bean.
Spoon fruit into the baked shell.
Place the remaining ⅓ cup sugar
in a small saucepan and heat
without stirring (shake pan instead) over moderately high heat
until sugar melts and turns am-
ber. Immediately pour over the
fruit, making a swirled pattern
on top. Let cool slightly, but
serve warm. Top with whipped
cream or ice cream. Makes 6 to 8
servings.

*Available frozen at specialty
food stores and well-stocked
supermarkets.

STRAWBERRY-KIWIFRUIT CHEESE TART

Press-in Pastry (follows)
8 ounces natural cream cheese, softened
¾ cup sugar
3 eggs
2 teaspoons grated lemon peel
½ cup fresh lemon juice
1 pint strawberries, hulled
2 kiwifruit, peeled and sliced
¼ cup apricot jam, pureed

Prepare Press-in Pastry. In a medium bowl beat cream cheese until creamy, then beat in sugar, eggs, lemon peel, and juice. Pour into baked tart shell and bake in a 350° F. oven 20 minutes, or until set; cool. Garnish the top with strawberries encircled with kiwifruit slices. Drizzle apricot puree over the fruits. Chill. Makes 8 servings.

PRESS-IN PASTRY In a medium bowl mix 1 cup all-purpose flour, ½ cup butter, 2 tablespoons confectioners' sugar, and 1 teaspoon grated lemon peel just until mixture is crumbly. Pat into the bottom and sides of an 11-inch fluted flan pan with removable bottom. Refrigerate 15 minutes to firm. Bake in a 425° F. oven 8 to 10 minutes, or until lightly browned.

VARIATION If desired, substitute blueberries or raspberries and sliced carambola or feijoa for the strawberries and kiwifruit.

BALI HAI MARZIPAN TART

Press-in Pastry (preceding recipe)
½ cup almond paste
¼ cup confectioners' sugar
2 tablespoons butter
1 egg white
¼ teaspoon almond extract
Assorted tropical fruit: papayas, feijoas, kiwifruit, carambolas, or mangoes (three or more fruits), peeled, seeded, if necessary, and sliced, to make 3 cups
¼ cup apricot jam, pureed
2 tablespoons chopped pistachios or chopped toasted almonds*

Prepare Press-in Pastry. In a medium bowl beat almond paste and sugar until smooth; beat in butter, egg white, and almond extract (if desired, use a food processor). Spread on baked tart shell. Arrange fruit decoratively in rings or spokes on top of filling. Drizzle puree over fruit and sprinkle with nuts; chill. Makes 8 servings.

*Toast almonds on a baking sheet in a 325° F. oven 8 to 10 minutes, or until lightly browned.

FRUIT-TOPPED TINY TARTS

1 can (8 ounces) almond paste
3 eggs
⅓ cup sugar
½ cup melted butter
¼ teaspoon almond extract
Unbaked Tart Shells (follows)
1½ cups fraises des bois, or 3 to 4 feijoas or carambolas, peeled, if necessary, and sliced
Confectioners' sugar
3 tablespoons chopped pistachio nuts

In a medium bowl beat almond paste with eggs and sugar until smooth. Mix in melted butter and almond extract. Fill Unbaked Tart Shells with almond mixture, place on a baking sheet, and bake in a 375° F. oven 15 minutes; cool. Top with berries, dust very lightly with confectioners' sugar (shaken through a sieve), and sprinkle with pistachios. Makes about 3 dozen tartlets.

UNBAKED TART SHELLS In a large bowl mix together until crumbly 1 cup plus 2 tablespoons softened butter, 6 tablespoons sugar, and 3 cups all-purpose flour. Add 2 eggs and mix until smooth. Shape into a ball. Pinch off pieces of dough and pat into 2-inch tart pans, pressing against bottoms and sides.

RHUBARB CUSTARD PIE

2 eggs
¾ cup sugar
½ teaspoon freshly grated
    nutmeg
2 teaspoons grated orange peel
2 tablespoons whipping cream
3 tablespoons all-purpose flour
¼ teaspoon salt
¼ teaspoon allspice
2 tablespoons melted butter
4 cups diced rhubarb stalks
Pastry dough from Rhubarb and
    Gooseberry Cobbler recipe
    (page 123)
Whipped cream for topping

In a large bowl beat eggs until
blended; mix in sugar, nutmeg,
orange peel, cream, flour, salt,
allspice, and butter. Add rhubarb, mixing to coat. Roll out
pastry on a floured board and fit
into a 9-inch pie pan. Flute
edges. Turn filling into the unbaked pastry shell. Bake in a
400° F. oven 15 minutes; reduce
temperature to 325° F. and bake
25 minutes longer. Cool to room
temperature. Serve with
whipped cream. Makes 8
servings.

AMARETTO CREAM TART

Butter Crust Shell (follows)
4 ounces natural cream cheese,
    softened
½ cup confectioners' sugar
2 tablespoons amaretto or Grand
    Marnier
1 cup whipping cream
Assorted fruit: mangoes, pa-
    payas, kiwifruit, carambolas,
    feijoas, peeled, seeded, if nec-
    essary, and sliced or halved
    strawberries or blueberries, to
    make about 2 cups
3 tablespoons melted currant
    jelly

Prepare Butter Crust Shell. In a
large bowl beat cream cheese
until creamy; beat in sugar and
liqueur. Add cream and whip until soft peaks form. Spread filling
in the cooled shell. Arrange fruit
in alternating concentric rings
on filling. Drizzle with melted
jelly. Refrigerate until serving
time. Makes 10 to 12 servings.

BUTTER CRUST SHELL In a medium bowl beat 1 cup unsifted
all-purpose flour, 2 tablespoons
confectioners' sugar, 1 teaspoon
grated lemon peel, and ½ cup
butter until mixture resembles
coarse meal. Pat into an 11-inch
fluted flan pan with removable
bottom, pressing against bottom
and sides. Bake in a 425° F. oven
8 to 10 minutes, or until shell is
lightly browned. Let cool.

ALMOND-PEAR TORTE

4 Red Bartlett pears, peeled,
    halved, cored, and sliced
½ cup water
¾ cup sugar
½ cup butter
2 eggs
⅞ cup ground almonds
1 tablespoon all-purpose flour
1 teaspoon grated orange peel
Vanilla ice cream or whipped
    cream for accompaniment

In a large covered skillet simmer
pears with water and ¼ cup of
the sugar 4 minutes. Remove
cover and cook about 4 minutes
longer, letting juices evaporate;
set aside. In a bowl beat butter
and remaining ½ cup sugar until
creamy. Beat in the eggs, nuts,
flour, and orange peel. Spread
batter in a buttered, floured 9-
inch springform pan. Arrange
pears in a pinwheel on top. Bake
in a 350° F. oven 30 minutes, or
until golden brown. Serve warm
with the ice cream or whipped
cream. Makes 8 servings.

ALMOND TORTE, RIO STYLE

5 eggs, separated
1 cup sugar
1 teaspoon grated lemon peel
½ teaspoon almond extract
1½ cups ground almonds or hazelnuts
¾ cup graham cracker or zwieback crumbs
1 teaspoon baking powder
½ teaspoon salt
1 cup whipping cream
Sugar to taste
Vanilla extract to taste
3 to 4 kiwifruit or feijoas, or 2 mangoes, peeled, seeded, if necessary, and sliced, or 2 cups fraises des bois

In a large bowl beat egg yolks until thick and pale in color, then gradually beat in sugar. Mix in lemon peel, almond extract, and ground almonds. In a separate bowl beat egg whites until soft peaks form; fold into yolks. Stir together graham cracker crumbs, baking powder, and salt, and gently fold into batter.

Butter and flour two 9-inch round cake pans. Pour in batter and spread. Bake in a 350° F. oven 25 minutes, or until layers are golden brown and tops spring back when lightly touched. Let cool slightly, then turn out onto racks and cool completely.

Whip cream until stiff and flavor to taste with sugar and vanilla. Place one cake layer on a serving plate and top with half the whipped cream. Cover with sliced fruit and a second cake layer and spread remaining cream on top. Decorate with fruit. Chill until serving time. Makes 12 servings.

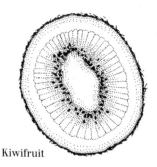
Kiwifruit

DEEP-DISH RHUBARB AND GOOSEBERRY COBBLER

Pastry (follows)
1 pint gooseberries
1½ cups diced rhubarb stalks
1⅓ cups sugar
3 tablespoons all-purpose flour
Pinch ground cinnamon
½ teaspoon grated lemon peel
Egg wash: 1 egg yolk beaten with 1 tablespoon water
Whipped cream or ice cream for topping (optional)

Prepare Pastry. In a medium bowl combine gooseberries and rhubarb. In a small bowl mix together sugar, flour, cinnamon, and lemon peel. Pour sugar mixture over fruit and mix lightly. Turn into a buttered 8-inch square baking dish. Roll out chilled pastry on a floured surface to a square slightly larger than 9 inches. Flip pastry onto waxed paper, then fit over top of baking dish. Peel off paper. Turn edges of pastry under and crimp. Make 2-inch slashes in pastry from just inside each corner diagonally toward center of cobbler. Brush pastry with egg wash. Bake in a 375° F. oven 45 to 50 minutes, or until golden brown. Let cool on a rack to room temperature. If desired, serve with whipped cream or ice cream. Makes 6 to 8 servings.

PASTRY Into a medium bowl sift together 1¼ cups all-purpose flour, 2 teaspoons sugar, ¼ teaspoon baking powder, and ¼ teaspoon salt. Cut in ½ cup chilled butter until mixture resembles coarse meal. In a small bowl beat together 1 egg yolk, 1 teaspoon vinegar, and 1 tablespoon cold water. Sprinkle liquid over flour mixture; toss lightly with a fork until mixture begins to come together, mixing as little as possible. Form dough into a loose ball, wrap in plastic wrap, and refrigerate 1 hour.

HAZELNUT ROULADE WITH CARAMBOLA

5 eggs, separated
¾ cup granulated sugar
½ cup graham cracker crumbs
1 teaspoon baking powder
¼ teaspoon almond extract
⅛ teaspoon *each* salt and cream of tartar
1 cup lightly packed ground or grated hazelnuts or almonds
1 cup whipping cream
2 tablespoons confectioners' sugar
1 tablespoon amaretto
2 ripe carambolas, feijoas, or kiwifruit

In a large bowl beat egg yolks until light and lemon-colored. Gradually beat in all except 2 tablespoons of the sugar and beat until thick and pale in color. Mix in crumbs, baking powder, and almond extract. Beat egg whites until foamy, add salt and cream of tartar, and beat until stiff. Beat in remaining 2 tablespoons sugar. Fold egg whites into the yolk mixture alternately with the ground nuts. Butter a 10- by 15-inch jelly-roll pan. Line bottom with waxed paper; butter again. Pour in batter and smooth evenly with a spatula. Bake in a 350° F. oven 20 minutes, or until the top of the cake springs back when touched lightly.

Let stand 5 minutes, then turn out onto a cloth dusted with confectioners' sugar. Gently roll up cloth and let cool on a rack.

For filling: Whip cream and 2 tablespoons confectioners' sugar until stiff. Stir in amaretto. Unroll cake and cover with two-thirds of the cream; roll up. Place on a serving platter. Spoon remaining cream down the center of the top. Slice carambolas or peel and slice feijoas or kiwifruit and arrange across the top. Makes 8 servings.

PAVLOVA

6 egg whites
¼ teaspoon *each* salt and cream of tartar
1½ cups granulated sugar
2 teaspoons vanilla extract
1 pint whipping cream
2 tablespoons confectioners' sugar
⅓ cup chopped toasted hazelnuts or macadamia nuts (optional)*
2 *each* sliced kiwifruit, feijoa, and carambola, *or* 1 mango, and 1 cup strawberries, hulled and sliced

In a medium bowl beat egg whites until foamy. Add salt and cream of tartar and beat until soft peaks form. Gradually add sugar, 1 tablespoon at a time, beating well after each addition. Add vanilla and beat until stiff and glossy. Spoon into a buttered 10-inch springform pan; make a depression in center. Bake in a 300° F. oven 1 hour, or until lightly browned; cool.

Whip cream until stiff; beat in confectioners' sugar. Fold in toasted nuts, if desired. Spoon into meringue shell, smoothing top. Arrange rings of fruit in concentric circles on top of whipped cream. Makes 8 to 10 servings.

*Toast nuts on a baking sheet in a 325° F. oven 8 to 10 minutes, or until lightly browned.

SOUFFLE CHEESECAKE WITH KIWIFRUIT

½ pint ricotta cheese
1 pound natural cream cheese, softened
6 eggs, separated
1 cup sugar
1 cup sour cream
2 tablespoons all-purpose flour
1 tablespoon brandy
1 teaspoon vanilla extract
1½ teaspoons grated lemon peel
Sliced kiwifruit, carambola, papaya, or whole raspberries for accompaniment

In a large mixing bowl beat the ricotta cheese and cream cheese until creamy; beat in the egg yolks, one at a time. Beat in ½ cup of the sugar, the sour cream, flour, brandy, vanilla, and lemon peel. In a medium bowl beat egg whites until soft peaks form; beat in the remaining sugar. Fold one-fourth of the egg whites into the cheese mixture, then fold in remaining egg whites. Turn into an ungreased 10-inch springform pan. Bake in a 325° F. oven 75 minutes, or until the center is set. Let cheesecake cool at room temperature, then chill. Serve cut in wedges with fruit alongside. Makes 12 servings.

SOUR CREAM SOUFFLE PANCAKES WITH FRUIT

6 eggs, separated
¼ cup sugar
1 cup sour cream
½ teaspoon salt
1 teaspoon grated lemon peel
½ cup unsifted all-purpose flour
Butter
Assorted fruit: kiwifruit, pepinos, and guavas, peeled and seeded, if necessary, and sliced, whole strawberries, raspberries, or blackberries, to make about 2 cups
Sour Cream Topping (follows)
Brown sugar for garnish

In a medium bowl beat egg whites until soft peaks form; beat in the sugar. Set aside. In a large bowl beat yolks until thick and light in color and beat in sour cream, salt, lemon peel, and flour, mixing until smooth. Fold in beaten egg whites. Melt 1 tablespoon butter in a large skillet and drop mounds of batter into pan forming 4-inch cakes. Brown on both sides. Serve topped with fruit and Sour Cream Topping. Sprinkle lightly with brown sugar. Makes 6 servings.

SOUR CREAM TOPPING In a small bowl stir together ½ cup sour cream, ¼ cup yogurt, 1 teaspoon grated lemon peel, and 1 teaspoon brown sugar.

LOQUAT BUCKLE

⅓ cup butter
¾ cup sugar
1 egg
1¾ cups all-purpose flour
1¾ teaspoons baking powder
¼ teaspoon salt
½ cup milk
10 to 12 loquats, halved, seeded, and sliced (about 2 cups)
Streusel Topping (follows)
Whipped cream or ice cream for topping

In a large bowl cream butter and sugar. Add egg; beat until light. Stir together the flour, baking powder, and salt. Add to creamed mixture alternately with milk. Pour batter into a greased 9-inch square pan. Arrange loquat slices in rows over batter. Sprinkle Streusel Topping over fruit. Bake in a 375° F. oven 45 minutes, or until browned. Serve warm or cold, cut into squares. Top with whipped cream or ice cream. Makes about 9 servings.

STREUSEL TOPPING In a medium bowl combine ½ cup packed brown sugar, ⅓ cup whole wheat flour, and ½ teaspoon ground cinnamon; cut in ¼ cup butter.

DUTCH BABIE WITH FRUIT AND ORANGE CREAM

2 tablespoons butter
4 eggs
1 cup milk
1 cup all-purpose flour
1 teaspoon grated orange peel
Mixed fruit: sliced kiwifruit, strawberries, feijoas, or mangoes, peeled and seeded, if necessary, and sliced, or blueberries and fraises des bois, to make 2 cups.
Orange Cream (follows)

Place butter in a 10-inch round baking pan and heat in a 425° F. oven until melted, about 5 minutes. Meanwhile, in a blender or food processor blend the eggs, milk, flour, and orange peel until smooth. Pour batter into the hot pan and bake in a 425° F. oven 20 to 25 minutes, or until puffed and golden brown. Cut in wedges and serve topped with mixed fruit and Orange Cream. Makes 4 brunch or dessert servings.

ORANGE CREAM In a medium bowl whip ½ cup whipping cream until stiff and fold in 1½ tablespoons thawed orange juice concentrate and 1 tablespoon honey.

CREME BRULEE SUPREME

2 cups half-and-half
1 cup whipping cream
6 egg yolks
½ cup sugar
1 teaspoon *each* grated lemon peel and vanilla extract
2 tablespoons orange-flavored liqueur, amaretto, or brandy
¾ cup packed light brown sugar (approximately)
2 cups fraises des bois, raspberries, sliced strawberries, or kiwifruit
Whipped cream for topping (optional)

In the top of a double boiler combine half-and-half and cream and heat over hot water until scalded. In a medium bowl beat egg yolks until pale and light in color, then beat in sugar and scalded cream. Return to top of double boiler and heat over simmering water, stirring, until custard thickens and coats a spoon, about 10 minutes. Remove from heat and stir in lemon peel, vanilla, and orange-flavored liqueur. Pour into a buttered 1½-quart ovenproof serving dish; cool and chill.

Sift brown sugar in an even layer over chilled custard, coating surface at least ¼ inch deep. Place custard in pan of crushed ice and broil just until sugar is caramelized, about 2 minutes. Cool and spoon over bowls of fraises des bois. Makes 6 servings.

PERSIMMON PUDDING

2 teaspoons baking soda
1 cup persimmon pulp
⅓ cup butter
1 cup sugar
1 egg
½ teaspoon vanilla extract
1⅓ cups all-purpose flour
1 teaspoon ground cinnamon
½ cup milk
½ cup chopped pecans
¾ cup raisins
Hard Sauce (follows)

Stir baking soda into persimmon pulp and set aside. In a medium bowl cream together the butter and sugar until light. Add egg and vanilla and beat until fluffy. In a small bowl stir together the flour and cinnamon. Add to the creamed mixture alternately with milk. Add persimmon pulp, nuts, and raisins; mix just until blended. Turn into a well-buttered and floured 1½-quart mold. Steam for 2 hours. Cool 10 minutes and unmold. Serve with Hard Sauce. Makes 8 servings.

HARD SAUCE Beat ½ cup butter until creamy and beat in 1¾ cups confectioners' sugar and 2 tablespoons brandy, beating until fluffy. Serve chilled or at room temperature.

COCONUT CREME CARAMEL

1 cup sugar
3½ cups milk
1 pint half-and-half
6 eggs
1 teaspoon vanilla extract
¾ cup shredded coconut
1 cup whipping cream
2 tablespoons rum or amaretto
1½ pints French vanilla ice
  cream

In a small, heavy saucepan heat
½ cup of the sugar until it melts
and caramelizes, shaking pan
frequently, about 5 minutes. At
once pour caramel into a 2-quart
mold and tilt the mold to coat all
sides.

In the pan used to make the
caramel, scald milk and half-
and-half. In a large bowl beat
eggs until light and beat in the
remaining ½ cup sugar. Stir in
hot milk, vanilla, and coconut.
Pour into the caramel-lined
mold, place in a pan containing
1 inch of hot water, and bake in a
350° F. oven 50 minutes, or until
the custard is set. Cool and chill.

With a sharp-pointed knife,
loosen the custard from the mold
and invert onto a large platter.
Pour the extra caramel syrup
into a bowl and reserve. Add 2
tablespoons water to mold and

heat to dissolve any remaining
caramel; add to reserved syrup.
Whip cream until stiff and flavor
with rum and ⅓ cup of caramel
syrup; turn into a bowl. Scoop
ice cream into balls and place in
a bowl. Serve wedges of custard
with ice cream balls and a dollop
of nougat whipped cream. Makes
8 to 10 servings.

OMELET FLAMBE WITH FRUITS

4 eggs, separated
¼ cup sugar
¾ teaspoon grated lemon peel
1 tablespoon cornstarch
Confectioners' sugar
2 tablespoons rum
Mixed fruit: kiwifruit, mangoes,
  carambolas, and/or feijoas,
  peeled, seeded, if necessary,
  and sliced, to make 2 cups

In a medium bowl beat egg
whites until soft peaks form; add
sugar, beating until stiff. In another bowl beat yolks until thick
and pale yellow in color; beat in
lemon peel and cornstarch. Fold
in the egg whites. Turn into a
buttered 10-inch ovenproof skillet or baking dish. Bake in a 375°
F. oven 25 minutes, or until
golden brown. Dust lightly with
confectioners' sugar. Warm rum,
ignite, and spoon, flaming, over
omelet. Serve on dessert plates
with fruit alongside. Makes 4
servings.

GINGERED MANGO SORBET

½ cup dry white wine
⅓ cup sugar
1½ tablespoons minced candied
  ginger
4 mangoes, peeled and diced
1 teaspoon grated lemon or lime
  peel
3 tablespoons fresh lemon or
  lime juice
Raspberry Puree (page 129),
  optional

In a medium saucepan combine wine, sugar, and ginger and cook until sugar is dissolved. Increase heat and boil 5 minutes; cool and chill. In a food processor or blender puree mangoes, lemon peel, and juice. Blend in cold syrup. Taste and add more minced candied ginger, if desired. Freeze in an ice cream maker following manufacturer's instructions. Serve sorbet scooped in ovals or rounds on Raspberry Puree, if desired. Makes about 1 quart.

PASSION FRUIT SORBET

½ cup sugar
¾ cup water
2 tablespoons orange-flavored
  liqueur
1 tablespoon fresh lime or lemon
  juice
¾ cup fresh orange juice
2 cups passion fruit puree
2 egg whites

In a small saucepan combine sugar and water; bring to a boil, reduce heat, and simmer 5 minutes; cool. Add liqueur, lime juice, orange juice, and passion fruit puree; blend. Pour into a metal pan and freeze until mushy. Turn into chilled bowl; add unbeaten egg whites and beat until light and fluffy. Or process in a food processor until fluffy. Return to a freezer container, cover, and freeze just until firm. If frozen solid, soften slightly in the refrigerator before serving. Makes 6 servings.

VARIATION Substitute 2 cups mango, feijoa, kiwifruit, sapote, or cherimoya puree for the passion fruit.

STRAWBERRY-MINT SORBET WITH FRAISES DES BOIS

1½ quarts strawberries, hulled
1 tablespoon minced fresh mint leaves
3 tablespoons fresh lemon juice
¾ cup sugar
¼ cup water
Fraises des bois or raspberries for garnish (about 2 cups)

In a food processor or blender puree strawberries, mint, and lemon juice. Combine sugar and water in a small saucepan and cook until it boils and sugar dissolves; cool syrup to room temperature. Add to berry puree.

Freeze in an ice cream maker following manufacturer's instructions. Serve while still softly mounding, topped with berries. Makes 6 servings.

VARIATION If desired, substitute 2 cups raspberries for 2 cups of the strawberries in the sorbet.

PAPAYA-HONEY SHERBET

1 large papaya or 2 large cherimoyas, peeled, seeded, and diced (about 2 cups)
1 cup fresh orange juice
2 tablespoons fresh lime or lemon juice
1 teaspoon grated lime or lemon peel
¼ cup honey
2 egg whites
1 lime, cut in wedges

In a blender puree papaya, orange juice, lime juice and peel, and honey. Pour into a freezer container and freeze until just solid. Remove from the freezer and turn into a medium bowl. Beat with an electric mixer, starting at low and gradually increasing to high speed, until smooth and slushy. In a large bowl beat egg whites until soft peaks form; fold in the papaya mixture. Turn into a freezer container, cover, and freeze until firm. Serve in dessert bowls or wine glasses and garnish with a lime wedge. Makes about 1 quart or 6 servings.

VARIATION Substitute 2 cups pureed prickly pear, cherimoya, passion fruit, or sapote for the papaya and add honey to taste.

SPICY GUAVA SORBET

1 tablespoon whole coriander seeds or pink peppercorns, crushed
½ cup sugar
1 cup water
2 cups guava or cherimoya puree
¼ teaspoon vanilla
2 tablespoons fresh lemon juice
1 teaspoon grated lemon peel
6 small nectarines (optional)
Mint sprigs for garnish

Place crushed coriander seeds or peppercorns in a medium saucepan with sugar and water; boil over medium heat until sugar is dissolved. Cool and chill. Add guava puree, vanilla, lemon juice, and lemon peel; mix well. Place in a shallow pan, cover, and freeze just until firm. Remove from pan to a food processor and process until thick and fluffy. Return to a freezer container, cover, and freeze until firm. Soften slightly in the refrigerator before serving. To serve, halve and pit nectarines if using, and place in dessert bowls. Top with a scoop of sorbet and garnish with mint. Makes 6 servings.

FRUIT SOUP WITH MINT ICE CREAM

Raspberry Puree (follows)
Crème Anglaise (follows)
2 cups milk
¼ cup packed chopped fresh
  mint leaves
6 egg yolks
¾ cup sugar
2 cups whipping cream
Assorted fruit: strawberries,
  blueberries, green grapes, kiwifruit, mangoes, carambolas
  peeled, seeded, if necessary,
  and sliced
Mint leaves for garnish

Prepare Raspberry Puree and
Crème Anglaise.

For ice cream: In the top of a
double boiler over hot water,
heat milk and mint until scalding; let stand 15 minutes. Puree
in a blender. In a medium bowl
beat egg yolks slightly; stir in
sugar and mint-infused milk.
Turn into the top of a double
boiler, place over hot water,
cook, stirring constantly, until
mixture thickens and coats a
spoon, about 10 minutes. Remove from heat and cool in a
pan of ice water; refrigerate until cold. Stir in cream. Freeze in
an ice cream maker following
manufacturer's instructions.

To assemble: Pour the Raspberry Puree and the Crème Anglaise into pitchers. Set out dinner plates, and simultaneously
pour each sauce onto half of one
plate, letting the sauces meet
down the center line. Place a
scoop of ice cream in the center
of the sauces. Repeat with remaining plates. Arrange fruit in
a pattern around ice cream,
placing strawberries, blueberries, and grapes on the Raspberry Puree, and kiwifruit,
mango, and carambola on the
Crème Anglaise. Garnish with
mint. Makes enough sauce and
ice cream for 6 servings.

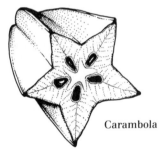

Carambola

RASPBERRY PUREE Thaw 1
package (10 ounces) frozen
raspberries, or use fresh raspberries and sweeten to taste. Puree in a food processor or
blender, then force through a
sieve, discarding seeds.

CRÈME ANGLAISE In the top of a
double boiler, heat 1 cup milk
over hot water until scalding. In
a small bowl beat 3 egg yolks until light and beat in 2 tablespoons
sugar. Pour in hot milk and turn
into the top of a double boiler.
Cook over hot water, stirring,
until custard coats a spoon. Remove from heat and stir in 1 tablespoon orange-flavored
liqueur.

VARIATION If desired, vary the
ice cream flavor by omitting the
mint and flavoring the cooked
custard with ¼ cup amaretto or
orange-flavored liqueur or 2 teaspoons vanilla extract.

PISTACHIO SPUMONE WITH FRUIT GARLAND

1 teaspoon butter
1 cup sugar
1/3 cup chopped pistachios, almonds, or hazelnuts
1/4 cup water
4 egg yolks
1 1/4 cups whipping cream
1 teaspoon vanilla extract
2 tablespoons Pernod or amaretto
Assorted fruits: kiwifruit, mangoes, papayas, carambolas, peeled and seeded, if necessary, and sliced, to make about 2 cups

In a skillet heat butter and 2 tablespoons of the sugar; add nuts. Sauté, stirring, until sugar melts and caramelizes and nuts turn golden, about 5 minutes. Turn out of pan onto a sheet of buttered foil and let cool; break apart.
In a small, heavy saucepan combine remaining sugar and water; boil until temperature registers 238° F. on a candy thermometer. Meanwhile, in a large bowl beat egg yolks until thick and pale yellow. Continuing to beat yolks, pour in hot syrup in a fine stream, beating until mixture cools to room temperature, about 7 minutes; chill. Whip cream until stiff; flavor with vanilla and liqueur. Fold cream and the nut crunch into egg mousse. Pour into a 1 1/2-quart mold. Cover and freeze until firm, at least 8 hours. To unmold, dip into a pan of hot water for 6 seconds, then invert onto a serving platter. Return to freezer 30 minutes to firm. To serve, garnish with a ring of fruits, or serve fruit in a bowl alongside. Makes 8 servings.

GRAND MARNIER ICE CREAM WITH FRUIT

3 1/2 cups milk
8 egg yolks
1 1/4 cups sugar
3 cups whipping cream
1/4 cup Grand Marnier or amaretto
2 to 3 cups fraises des bois, raspberries, blueberries, or peeled, sliced kiwifruit or feijoas

In the top of a double boiler over hot water, scald milk. In a medium bowl beat egg yolks, then beat in sugar until light in color. Pour in hot milk, return to top of double boiler, and cook until thickened and custard coats a spoon, about 10 minutes. Cool in a pan of ice water; chill. Stir in cream and liqueur. Churn in an ice cream maker following manufacturer's instructions. Turn into a container and freeze. To serve, scoop into balls in dessert bowls or wine goblets and top with fruit. Makes about 10 servings.

RED BANANA FUDGE SPLITS

4 ounces semisweet chocolate, cut up
1/3 cup half-and-half or coffee
1/4 cup light corn syrup
4 Red Cuban bananas
1 pint vanilla, toasted almond, or pecan ice cream
1/4 cup chopped toasted almonds or pecans*

In the top of a double boiler place the chocolate, half-and-half, and corn syrup. Heat over hot water, stirring, until smoothly blended; set aside. When ready to serve, peel and slice the bananas diagonally and arrange in dessert bowls, points outward. Scoop ice cream into balls and nestle a ball in the center of each banana "boat." Spoon over hot fudge sauce and sprinkle with nuts. Makes 4 servings.

*Toast almonds on a baking sheet in a 325° F. oven 8 to 10 minutes, or until lightly browned.

MACADAMIA-MANGO SUNDAE

½ cup unsalted chopped macadamia nuts or Brazil nuts
1 tablespoon butter
½ cup unsifted confectioners'
 sugar
½ cup whipping cream
1 tablespoon dark rum
2 mangoes or 3 kiwifruit
1 pint vanilla ice cream

In a small saucepan sauté nuts
in butter until lightly browned.
Blend in confectioners' sugar,
cream, and rum. Boil over medium-high heat, stirring constantly, until sauce thickens and
glistens, about 3 minutes. Remove from heat. Peel, seed, and
slice mangoes into dessert
bowls. Top with a scoop of ice
cream. Spoon over the hot nut
sauce. Makes 4 servings.

FRUITS ROMANOFF

1 cup whipping cream
3 tablespoons kirsch, Grand
 Marnier, or Cointreau
2 tablespoons confectioners'
 sugar
½ cup toasted slivered almonds*
½ cup crushed almond macaroons (optional)
1 pint vanilla ice cream, slightly
 softened
Sliced kiwifruit, mangoes, whole
 raspberries or strawberries, or
 a combination (2 to 3 cups)

In a large bowl whip cream until
stiff; stir in liqueur and confectioners' sugar. Fold in almonds
and macaroons. Turn ice cream
into a bowl and fold in whipped
cream mixture. Cover and freeze
about 1 hour, or until just firm.
To serve, spoon fruit into dessert
bowls and top with a spoonful of
sauce. Makes 6 servings.

*Toast almonds on a baking
sheet in a 325° F. oven 8 to 10
minutes, or until lightly
browned.

PRICKLY PEAR ICICLES

2 cups prickly pear puree (see
 Note)
3 tablespoons fresh lime juice
1 cup water
¼ cup sugar or to taste

In a food processor or blender
combine the prickly pear puree,
lime juice, water, and sugar.
Turn into ice cube trays, insert
sticks, and freeze until firm.
Serve popsicle style. Makes
about 1 dozen.

NOTE To prepare cactus for pureeing, cover fruit with boiling
water for 5 minutes; drain. If
fruit still has stickers, hold with
tongs and peel with a sharp
knife. Cut peeled fruit in half
and scoop out seeds with a
spoon.

FRESH FRUIT AND SAUCES

ORIENTAL COMPOTE

⅓ cup sugar
⅓ cup water
2 tablespoons fresh lime juice
1 teaspoon chopped candied ginger or grated fresh ginger root
2 carambolas, thinly sliced and seeded
2 tangerines, peeled and separated into sections
¾ cup peeled, thinly sliced jícama or seeded litchis
1 cup seedless grapes or peeled, seeded, and diced chayote
Blossoms or mint sprigs for garnish

In a small saucepan make a syrup by boiling together the sugar and water until sugar is dissolved; stir in lime juice and ginger. Cool. Place in a bowl the carambolas, tangerines, jícama, and grapes. Pour over syrup and chill 1 hour. Serve in bowls garnished with a blossom or mint sprig. Makes 4 servings.

KIWIFRUIT AND MELON BALL COUPE

½ cup sugar
⅓ cup water
1 tablespoon lemon peel or lime peel
¼ cup fresh lemon or lime juice
¼ cup rum
4 kiwifruit, peeled and sliced
1 quart assorted melon balls (honeydew, cantaloupe, crenshaw, and watermelon)
Mint sprigs or blossoms for garnish

In a small saucepan combine sugar and water. Bring to a boil; reduce heat, and simmer 3 minutes. Stir in lemon peel, juice, and rum; cool. Pour lemon-rum syrup over kiwifruit and melon balls; chill. To serve, spoon fruits and syrup into serving bowls. Garnish with mint or a blossom. Makes 6 servings.

VARIATION Instead of the melon balls, substitute a combination of sliced papaya, mango, feijoa, and carambola.

CARAMBOLA AND PAPAYA FRUIT BOWLS

1 carambola, sliced
1 papaya, peeled, seeded, and diced
1 cup seedless red or green grapes
1 cup strawberries, hulled
3 tablespoons orange-flavored liqueur
½ teaspoon grated lemon or lime peel
Fresh mint sprigs for garnish

In a medium bowl place the carambola, papaya, grapes, and berries. Stir together the liqueur and citrus peel and pour over. Chill 1 hour. Spoon into bowls and garnish with mint. Makes 4 servings.

VARIATION Another season, utilize fruits such as nectarines, peaches, and raspberries, or add sliced Granny Smith apples or Red Bartlett pears at the last minute.

CARIBBEAN FRUIT PLATE WITH HONEY-ORANGE CREAM

Honey-Orange Cream (follows)
1 large mango, peeled, seeded, and sliced
2 feijoas, peeled and sliced
2 kiwifruit, peeled and sliced
2 Red Cuban bananas, peeled and sliced
1 small pineapple, quartered, cored, peeled, and sliced
Fresh mint sprigs or blossoms for garnish

Prepare Honey-Orange Cream. Arrange the sliced fruit on a large platter. Garnish with mint or blossoms. Pass Honey-Orange Cream. Makes 6 servings.

HONEY-ORANGE CREAM In a small bowl beat 2 eggs until light in color; beat in ¼ cup honey, 3 tablespoons fresh lime juice, ½ cup fresh orange juice, and 2 teaspoons grated orange peel. Pour into the top of a double boiler, place over hot water, and cook, stirring, until sauce is thickened, about 10 minutes. Cool and chill. In a small bowl beat 1 cup whipping cream until stiff and fold into the honey sauce. Spoon into a serving container, cover, and refrigerate.

AMARETTO CREAM WITH TROPICAL FRUITS

⅔ cup packed light brown sugar
1 package (1 tablespoon) unflavored gelatin
2 cups milk
4 egg yolks
¼ cup amaretto or rum
1 teaspoon vanilla extract
1 cup whipping cream
Raspberry Puree (page 129)
2 cups sliced kiwifruit, mangoes, carambolas, or bananas

In the top of a double boiler mix together the sugar, salt, and gelatin. Stir in milk. Place over hot water and heat until scalded. Beat egg yolks until light; pour in part of the milk mixture and return to the top of the double boiler. Cook, stirring, until thickened, about 10 minutes. Remove from heat and stir in liqueur and vanilla. Cool, then chill until syrupy, about 45 minutes. In a medium bowl whip cream until stiff; fold into egg mixture. Turn into individual dessert bowls or a 1½-quart mold. Cover and chill. Unmold and serve with Raspberry Puree and fruits. Makes 6 to 8 servings.

PRICKLY PEAR SAUCE

¼ cup sugar
1 tablespoon cornstarch
1 cup prickly pear puree (page 66)
1 tablespoon amaretto
2 tablespoons fresh lemon juice

In a medium saucepan combine the sugar, cornstarch, and puree. Cook, stirring, until slightly thickened and clear, about 5 minutes. Stir in amaretto and lemon juice and cook a few minutes longer. Serve over ice cream, sorbet, or custard. Makes 1¼ cups.

VARIATION Substitute passion fruit puree for the prickly pear.

GRAND MARNIER SAUCE FOR FRUITS

1 cup sour cream
1 teaspoon grated lemon peel
½ cup confectioners' sugar
2 tablespoons Grand Marnier or amaretto
Fruits: peeled, sliced kiwifruit, mangoes, feijoas, sapotes

In a medium bowl blend together the sour cream, lemon peel, sugar, and liqueur. Spoon into a serving bowl, cover, and chill. Spoon over fruit arranged in wine goblets or pretty dessert bowls. Makes about 1½ cups sauce or 6 servings.

DOWN UNDER FRUIT COCKTAIL

¾ cup cape gooseberries, each
  berry halved
1 cup diced fresh pineapple
1 cup diced papaya or mango
1 kiwifruit, peeled and sliced
2 tablespoons orange-flavored
  liqueur or orange juice concentrate, thawed
1 teaspoon chopped fresh mint

In a medium bowl place the cape
gooseberries, pineapple, papaya,
and kiwifruit. Spoon over liqueur
and mint and mix lightly; chill 1
hour. Makes 4 servings.

ASIAN PEAR AND FETA PLATE

2 Asian pears, peeled, seeded,
  and sliced
2 ounces feta cheese, crumbled
1 tablespoon chopped fresh mint
  leaves
1 tablespoon chopped pistachio
  nuts

On each of two dessert plates arrange the pear slices in a fan
shape. Sprinkle with feta, mint,
and pistachios. Makes 2
servings.

NOTE Instead of the Asian pears,
substitute 1 mango, peeled,
seeded, and sliced.

RHUBARB-STRAWBERRY FOOL

¾ pound rhubarb, leaves
  trimmed away and discarded
  and stalks cut in ½-inch pieces
2 cups strawberries, hulled and
  sliced
½ cup sugar
1½ cups whipping cream
1 teaspoon vanilla extract or 1
  tablespoon amaretto
Fresh mint sprigs for garnish

In a large saucepan place rhubarb and strawberries with
sugar and let stand for 10 minutes. Cook over medium heat,
stirring occasionally, until tender, about 10 minutes. Remove
from heat, cover, and chill. To
serve, whip cream until stiff and
stir in vanilla or amaretto. In
parfait glasses alternate the rhu-
barb-berry sauce and cream.
Garnish with a mint sprig.

VARIATION If desired, omit
cream and spoon fruit sauce
over balls of vanilla or pecan ice
cream.

ZABAGLIONE WITH FRUIT

6 egg yolks
6 tablespoons sugar
½ cup dry white wine
1 teaspoon grated lemon peel
4 kiwifruit, peeled and sliced, or
  2 cups fraises des bois
Whipped cream for garnish
  (optional)

In the top of a double boiler beat
egg yolks until light; beat in
sugar, wine, and lemon peel.
Place over hot water and beat
with a wire whip or portable
electric beater until it triples in
volume and holds a peak, about
7 minutes. Cool immediately by
setting in a pan of ice water;
chill. Arrange fruit in wine goblets and spoon over sauce. If desired, top with whipped cream.
Makes 4 servings.

VARIATION Substitute feijoa or
mango and a few raspberries or
blueberries for color and tang.

FROZEN PERSIMMONS WITH LIQUEUR

Freeze persimmons whole. To
serve, slice off the stem end and
serve upright with a drizzle of
Grand Marnier or dark rum.
Garnish with a cyclamen
blossom.

BAKED PAPAYA WITH VANILLA BEAN

3 small papayas
1 piece (6 inches) vanilla bean, cut into 1-inch lengths
½ cup fresh coconut milk (page 50)
1 lime, cut in wedges for garnish
Flower blossoms: baby orchids or cyclamen for garnish

Halve the papayas and scoop out the seeds. Place the halves on a baking pan. Split open the pieces of vanilla bean, scraping a few seeds into each papaya half and dropping in a piece of the pod as well. Spoon in some coconut milk. Cover with foil and bake in a 375° F. oven 10 to 15 minutes, or until heated through. Serve each half on a dessert plate, garnished with a wedge of lime and a blossom. Makes 6 servings.

BAKED QUINCE AND APPLE SLICES

2 quinces, peeled, cored, and sliced
3 apples, peeled, cored, and sliced
½ cup sugar
½ cup water
2 teaspoons grated orange peel
Whipped cream for topping (optional)

In a buttered casserole or baking dish place the quinces and apples; sprinkle with sugar. Pour over water and scatter over peel. Cover and bake in a 375° F. oven until tender, about 45 minutes to 1 hour. Cool or chill. Serve with whipped cream. Makes 4 to 6 servings.

RED BANANA FRITTERS

1 cup all-purpose flour
1 egg
1 tablespoon butter, melted
¼ teaspoon *each* salt and sugar
½ cup beer
4 Red Cuban bananas
Oil for frying
Confectioners' sugar
Honey-Orange Cream (page 133)

In a food processor or blender process the flour, egg, butter, salt, sugar, and beer until smooth. Let stand, covered, 2 hours before using. Peel bananas and cut into ¾-inch slices. Dip in batter and fry in deep fat (370° F.) until golden, about 2 to 3 minutes. Drain on paper towels and dust with confectioners' sugar. Serve warm with Honey-Orange Cream. Makes 4 servings.

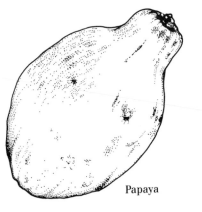

Papaya

FRUIT-TOPPED CHEESE WITH FRUIT SAUCES

This party idea is designed for a crowd. Arrange 1 or 2 small Brie and a St. André on a board or individual plates. Shape mascarpone cheese into a loaf and place alongside. Top the cheeses with various combinations of fruit. Use spokes of raspberries and blackberries on one; top another with green grapes and encircle with slices of kiwifruit; arrange fans of sliced mango and nectarine plus slices of kiwifruit on another and encircle with toasted pine nuts. Stud the mascarpone cheese with raspberries.

Have ready several dessert fruit sauces, made by pureeing such fruits as peach, mango, papaya, blackberry, strawberry, and raspberry (straining seeds, if necessary). Sweeten to taste. Have a basket of sliced baguettes alongside.

Let guests choose their cheese and fruit sauce combinations to spread and spoon over sliced bread for an outdoor appetizer and wine party. Or for a dessert event, omit bread and serve cheese in small wedges on plates and top with fruit sauce.

CONTINENTAL CHEESE WITH KIWIFRUIT, FEIJOA, AND BERRIES

1 pound natural cream cheese, softened
¼ cup unsifted confectioners' sugar
⅓ cup whipping cream
1½ teaspoons grated lemon peel
2 tablespoons Cointreau or Grand Marnier
2 ripe kiwifruit, peeled and sliced
2 ripe feijoas, peeled and sliced
1 cup raspberries or strawberries, hulled and halved

In a medium bowl beat cream cheese until creamy; beat in sugar, cream, lemon peel, and liqueur. Line a 1-pint mold (such as a heart, flower, or pyramid) with a double layer of cheesecloth. Spoon in the cheese mixture, smooth top and arrange cheesecloth over the top. Cover and chill (up to 2 days).

Unmold on a platter, ring with kiwifruit, feijoa, and berries. Makes 8 servings.

MANGO DAIQUIRI

1 small mango, peeled, seeded, and diced (about ¾ cup)
⅓ cup fresh lime juice
3 tablespoons sugar
⅓ cup rum
4 cups crushed ice
Lime slices for garnish

In a blender puree the mango, lime juice, sugar, and rum. Add ice, a small amount at a time, blending until frothy. Pour into glasses and garnish with a lime slice. Makes 3 to 4 drinks.

VARIATION Omit rum and substitute 3 tablespoons tequila and 2 tablespoons orange-flavored liqueur. Dip rims of glasses in water, then into a small dish of salt. Pour in beverage.

PAPAYA SMOOTHIE

1 medium papaya, peeled, seeded, and cut into pieces
1 banana, peeled
1 cup plain yogurt
2 tablespoons fresh lime juice
1 tablespoon honey
½ cup chopped ice
2 tablespoons sunflower seeds or shredded coconut (optional)

In a blender puree the papaya, banana, yogurt, lime juice, honey, ice, and sunflower seeds. Pour into 12-ounce glasses and serve. Makes 2 servings.

BIBLIOGRAPHY

Beck, Bruce. *Produce.* New York: Friendly Press, Inc., 1984.

Brouck, B. *Plants Consumed by Man.* London: Academic Press, 1975.

Dahlen, Martha, and Phillipps, Karen. *Chinese Vegetables.* New York: Crown Publishers, Inc., 1983.

Ensminger, Audrey H., Ensminger, M.E., Konlande, James E., and Robson, John R.K., M.D. *Foods and Nutrition Encyclopedia.* Clovis, CA: Pegus Press, 1983.

Hillman, Howard. *The Cook's Book.* New York: Avon Books, 1981.

Kluger, Marilyn. *The Wild Flavor.* New York: Coward, McCann and Geoghegan, Inc., 1970.

Larkcom, Joy. *The Salad Garden.* New York: The Viking Press, 1984.

Marteka, Vincent. *Mushrooms: Wild and Edible.* New York: W.W. Norton & Co., 1980.

Martin, Franklin W. *Handbook of Tropical Food Crops.* Boca Raton, FL: CRC Press, Inc., 1984.

Masefield, G.B., Wallis, M., Harrison, S.G., and Nicholson, B.E. *The Oxford Book of Food Plants.* London: Oxford University Press, 1969.

Miller, Carey D., Bazore, Katherine, and Bartow, Mary. *Fruits of Hawaii.* Honolulu: The University Press of Hawaii, 1981.

Ortiz, Elizabeth Lambert. *The Book of Latin American Cooking.* New York: Alfred A. Knopf, 1979.

Root, Waverley. *Food.* New York: Simon and Schuster, 1980.

Sunset New Western Garden Book. Menlo Park, CA: Lane Publishing Co., 1979.

Tate, Joyce L. *Cactus Cook Book.* Reseda, CA: Cactus and Succulent Society of America, Inc., 1971.

Yamaguchi, Mas. *World Vegetables: Principles, Production and Nutritive Values.* Westport, CT: AVI Publishing Company, 1983.

SEED SOURCES

W. ATLEE BURPEE CO.
300 Park Avenue
Warminster, Pennsylvania 18991

THE COOK'S GARDEN
Box 65050
Londonderry, Vermont 05148

GLECKLER'S SEEDMEN
Metamora, Ohio 43540

HARRIS SEEDS
3670 Buffalo Road
Rochester, New York 14624

HORICULTURAL ENTERPRISES
Box 810082
Dallas, Texas 75381

JOHNNY'S SELECTED SEEDS
299 Foss Hill Road
Albion, Maine 04910

LE MARCHE SEEDS
INTERNATIONAL
P.O. Box 566
Dixon, California 95620

MUSHROOMPEOPLE
P.O. Box 158
Inverness, California 94937

NICHOLS GARDEN NURSERY
1190 North Pacific Highway
Albany, Oregon 97321

GEO. W. PARK SEED CO., INC.
Highway 254 North
Greenwood, South Carolina
29647

THE PEPPER GAL
10536 119 Avenue North
Largo, Florida 33543

SHEPHERD'S GARDEN SEEDS
7389 West Zayante Road
Felton, California 95018

STOKES SEEDS
1436 Stokes Building
Buffalo, New York 14240

SUNRISE ORIENTAL SEED CO.
Box 10058
Elmwood, Connecticut 06110

THOMPSON & MORGAN INC.
Box 1308
Jackson, New Jersey 08527

INDEX

RECIPE INDEX

INDEX TO FRUITS AND VEGETABLES

BIOGRAPHICAL NOTES

Lou Pappas' interest in fresh produce goes back to her childhood in the Willamette Valley of Oregon, where a favorite pastime was picking wild berries. After graduating from Oregon State University in home economics with a minor in journalism, she moved to California and became accustomed to eating freshly picked fruits, vegetables and herbs from her garden. A former food consultant for *Sunset* magazine, she presently is food editor of the *Peninsula Times Tribune* in Palo Alto, California. She has also published articles in such magazines as *Gourmet* and *Cuisine* and is the author of sixteen cookbooks. Her most recent works include *New American Chefs* and *Entertaining in the Light Style* (both from 101 Productions) and *Vegetable Cookery* (HP Books).

Although a picky eater as a child, Jane Horn never had to be coaxed to eat fresh fruits and vegetables. They tasted good to her then and still do now. One of the pleasures of living in California for this native New Yorker is the diversity of fresh produce routinely available to her at neighborhood markets. She is a cookbook writer and editor, with a master's degree in communication from Stanford University. Her most recent collaborations include a poultry cookbook published as part of the new California Culinary Academy series (Ortho Books), and *California Fresh*, a cookbook by The Junior League of Oakland–East Bay. She lives near San Francisco, in Piedmont, California, with her husband, Barry, a physician, and their two children.